An Essential Guide to Cybersecurity

What You Need to Know

Written by David Miller, B.S. M.S.

Edited by Veronica Miller, B.S. M.S.

Table of Contents

About the Author

David Miller is an instructional designer in Tampa, Florida. He was educated at home by his mother, a certified teacher and experienced instructional designer. From kindergarten to high school, David was exposed to a technology-rich learning environment with a diverse curriculum. In addition to classroom instruction he had the opportunity to learn from using the computer, the Internet, CDs, field trips and self-directed projects. At fifteen David took the SAT examination and scored high enough to be accepted at most universities. But based on parental advice he enrolled at Hillsborough Community College to begin his undergraduate education. Upon graduation from the University of South Florida he received a Bachelor's Degree in Information Technology. After obtaining his first degree, David decided to pursue a master's degree in the field of education; specifically to design educational courses and programs. He selected Walden University and enrolled in the fall of 2011. In January 2014, David graduated with an MS in Instructional Design and Technology. To date he works in instructional design/e-learning industry as an independent contractor, and has designed several courses for in class and online delivery. He has also authored technical books.

 Trinity Technology and Media
524 Royal Greens Drive
Temple Terrace, FL 33617

Website: http://www.trinitytechnologymedia.com/

Facebook: http://www.facebook.com/trinitytechnologymedia

E-Mail: trinityt@trinitytechnologymedia.com

Alternate E-Mail: DMill8823@aol.com

Purpose of this Book

People have become increasingly connected online and through mobile devices in various aspects of their lives. Therefore, having proper and effective cybersecurity has become paramount, especially over the last few years. With the availability of social security numbers, date of births, bank accounts, and financial information online, identity theft is a painful reality for people across the world. Hackers and phishers are always on the prowl in the current social media era. Additionally, our recent presidential election showed how vulnerable governmental online databases and systems really are.

This book is intended to inform users, employees, and business owners how they can best protect themselves from cyber criminals and the precautions that should be taken. You will also read about how cybersecurity is (and should be) enforced in various fields, and important updates on advancements made in cybersecurity.

Here are the objectives upon completion of this book:

- Learn about the history, definition, emergence and importance of cybersecurity.
- Be aware of the various types of cybercrimes.
- Read important news and statistics regarding hacking, espionage, phishing, etc.
- Protect your mobile devices and social media accounts.
- Differentiate between cybersecurity and network security.

I hope that you will have a productive and rewarding experience learning and reading about the increasingly vital topic of cybersecurity.

Chapter 1
What is Cybersecurity?

Section Topics

❖ History

❖ Definition

❖ Emergence

❖ Importance

History

Beginning in the 1970s, the exploration of then-emerging telecommunications technology began. The first modern day hackers appeared as they attempted to sidestep the system by making free phone calls, a practice that was defined as "phreaking", pioneered by John Draper, a.k.a. Captain Crunch. Draper was later arrested and convicted on charges related to his nefarious phreaking activities multiple times. By 1986, malware (short for malicious software), in the form of the first virus, "Brain", took shape, the same year that the Computer Fraud and Abuse Act was instituted. It prohibits unauthorized access or damage of protected computers. Two years later, the Morris worm followed, named after Robert Morris. The virus was so severe and spread so rapidly that it successfully shut down much of the internet. The Morris worm was a landmark incident as the first widespread instance of a denial-of-service (DoS), cybersecurity attack. Fortunately, due to the infancy of the internet at the time, the impact was not as devastating as it would have been today. But it paved the way for the numerous kinds of security issues that have emerged in the decades since. A computer hacker and fugitive named Kevin Poulsen, was featured on America's Most Wanted, and was arrested in 1991. However, since his release from prison, he reinvented himself as a journalist and contributed to the online computer security news portal SecurityFocus. In the years to follow, viruses and attacks such as backdoors, denial-of-service attacks, direct-access attacks, eavesdropping, spoofing, tampering, privilege escalation, phishing, clickjacking, and social engineering all emerged.

The first decade of the 21st Century saw malicious Internet activity become a major criminal enterprise, as adware and spyware emerged with programs such as Conducent, TimeSink, Aureate/Radiate and Comet Cursor. Malware also appeared, with big-name threats such as Code Red, Nimda, Welchia, Slammer and Conficker all wreaking havoc on unprotected machines. AOL suffered through the first real phishing attacks, with fraudsters stealing users' credentials. Today, phishing attacks have become increasingly mainstream, with online banking and social networking sites. Zero day attacks, ransomware, rogue antispyware, clickfraud, government attacks, and other attacks have all made their mainstream debut in the current decade.

The Morris worm and other early nuisance attacks ultimately led to the development of the security industry including the establishment of CERTs (Computer Emergency Response Teams) for coordinating responses to these kinds of emergencies, and preventative and detective security products. There has also been further development of antivirus technology in order to spot the signature of the virus and prevent it from executing. These threats have played an integral role in driving the awareness of computer users of the risks of reading emails from untrusted and unreliable sources, and opening their attachments (which lead to the establishment of spam). Companies began to realize that if viruses were to spread from corporate email accounts, questions about the security and integrity of that company would likely be brought into the public eye.

Definition

Computer security, also known as cyber security or IT security is defined as the protection of information systems from any theft or damage to hardware, software, as well as interference in the services that they provide. Cybersecurity is the overall process of utilizing security measures for data confidentiality, integrity, and availability. It protects assets such as data on computers, servers, and cloud technology from hackers and unauthorized access. There is protection against physical access to hardware, and attacks via network access, data and code injection. It is the body of technologies, processes and practices designed to protect networks, computers, programs and data from attack, damage or unauthorized access. In a computing context, the term security implies cybersecurity. The goal of cybersecurity is to protect and ensure security of data. Some of the measures include access control, awareness training, risk assessment, security assessment, vulnerability management, etc. Cybersecurity functions are critical because web servers open windows between individual networks and the entire world virtually. Server maintenance, web application updates and website coding help to determine the degree of web security needed. Benefits of these processes involve protecting information and systems from major threats, such as cyber terrorism, cyber warfare, and cyber espionage.

Computer security is the generic name for the collection of tools that protects data and thwarts hackers. Network security measures are needed to protect data during their transmission (physical transfer of data) and to guarantee that data transmissions are authentic. The essential technology for most network and computer security applications is called encryption. Application security, information security, network security, disaster recovery, business continuity planning, and end-user education are important facets of cybersecurity. Network security threats usually fall into two categories. These are passive threats, sometimes referred to as eavesdropping, which involve attempts by an attacker to obtain communication information, and active threats, which entail modification of the transmitted data or the creation of false transmissions.

Websites are usually prone to security risks, in addition to networks where web servers are connected. Furthermore, even the most robust or up-to-date programs and databases either have bugs and/or weaknesses to varying degrees. These tools are all inherently complex. Poorly written software exacerbates security issues, and the bugs help to create web security issues that directly affect web applications and the server. Faulty software increases vulnerability, which is a system susceptibility or flaw. Ensuring cybersecurity requires coordinated efforts throughout an information system.

A message, file, document, or other collection of data is said to be authentic when it is genuine and came from its alleged source. Message authentication is a procedure that allows communicating parties to verify that messages are authentic. The two important aspects of verification are whether the contents of the message haven't been altered and that the source is authentic. There is also the modification of messages, where a portion of a legitimate message is altered, and messages are delayed or reordered, to produce an unauthorized effect. For example, a message meaning "Allow John Smith to read confidential file accounts" can be modified to mean "Allow Fred Brown to read confidential file accounts".

A masquerade takes place when one entity pretends to be a different entity. Encryption protects against masquerades and passive attacks (eavesdropping). There are different requirements required to protect against active attacks (falsification of data and transactions). Protection against such attacks is known as message authentication.

Most threats to Wifi networks come from rogue users, which refers to any unauthorized user in the wireless domain that interferes in the network and receives transmissions. Rogue access points (or rogue APs) can be broadcasted outside a business, and makes access available to outsiders. Anyone with wireless access on a laptop, smartphone, or tablet can receive access from the parking lot. When connected to an open network without password requirement, the data that flows between the device and the wireless router is unencrypted.

Another one of the major security threats to consider is the "man in the middle" (MITM) attack, which is the most advanced type of wireless network attack. This attack occurs when the attacker affects the message between the user and an access point. The message can be read and intercepted, and possibly changed to display wrong information.

Emergence

For most of the 1970s and 1980s, threats to computer security had already existed. However, these threats were in the form of malicious insiders reading documents without permission. Computer security largely revolved around governance risk and compliance (GRC), and evolved separately from the history of computer security software. Network breaches and malware were present and were used for maliciously during the early history of computers. The Russians began to deploy cyber warfare, which has evolved into a major security threat (and successful operation) today. In 1986, German computer hacker Marcus Hess successfully hacked an internet gateway in Berkeley, and was able to use that connection to piggyback (tag along for entrance to an access point) on the Arpanet. He was able hack into 400 military computers, including Pentagon mainframes. The intent was to steal and sell the Pentagon's secrets to the KGB. He was only caught when an astronomer detected the intrusion.

From this point onward, in the history of cybersecurity, computer viruses began to become more of a serious threat. Increasing network connectivity was breeding ground for viruses such as the Morris worm. Therefore, antivirus software was established in response; the first program was created in 1987. After the Morris worm, viruses become even more deadly and dangerous, affecting an increasing number of systems. The worm set the template for the era of massive internet outages in which we live.

Russian security services have organized a number of Denial-of-Service (DoS) attacks as a part of their cyber warfare against other countries. In 2007, there where cyberattacks on Estonia, and in 2008, the same occurred on Russia, South Ossetia, Georgia, and Azerbaijan. One identified young Russian hacker was reportedly paid by Russian state security services to hack into NATO computers. In April 2015, CNN reported that Russian hackers had successfully penetrated sensitive parts of the White House computers. The FBI, the Secret Service, and other U.S. intelligence agencies defined the attacks as among the most sophisticated ever launched against U.S. government systems. During that same year, CNN reported that hackers likely working for the Russian government, are suspected in the State Department hack. Federal law enforcement, intelligence and congressional officials briefed on the investigation say the hack of the State email system is the "worst ever" cyberattack intrusion against a federal agency.

By 2016, Russian cyber warfare was in full effect, especially in the elections. A senior Kremlin advisor and top cyber official stated at a Russian national security conference that the country was working on new strategies for the information arena equivalent to testing a nuclear bomb. The release of hacked emails belonging to the Democratic National Committee, John Podesta, and General Colin Powell were provided via DCLeaks and WikiLeaks, with the assistance of Russian aides. The hacking was a deliberate attempt at undermining Democratic presidential candidate Hillary Clinton, as well as the proliferation of political propaganda and "fake news" on major social media portals.

Importance

Cybersecurity is one of the most urgent issues of today, with computer networks always being targeted by criminals. The danger of cyber security breaches will only increase as these networks expand. The necessity for strong cybersecurity measures is self-evident. In recent years, there has been a proliferation of cyberattacks that have wreaked havoc on companies, governments and individuals. One of the most problematic and insidious elements of cybersecurity is the quickly and constantly evolving nature of security risks. Cyber risk has been established at the top of the international agenda, as high-profile breaches (i.e. WikiLeaks) have raised fears that hack attacks and other security failings could endanger the global economy.

The U.S. federal government has allotted over $13 billion annually to cyber security since late 2010. The Global Risks 2015 report stated that 90 percent of companies worldwide recognize they are insufficiently prepared to protect themselves against cyber attacks. Cyber crime (explained in further detail in Chapter 3) costs the global economy over US$400 billion per year, according to the Center for Strategic and International Studies. Furthermore, in 2013, approximately 3,000 companies in the United States had their systems compromised by criminals. High-profile US retailers Target and Home Depot were among many organizations that has lost customer data and credit card information. In other companies, money from accounts have been stolen, industrial espionage has occurred, and in some cases, the cyber thieves even took over company systems and demanded ransom money to unlock them.

 Governments and businesses around the world are constantly searching for better cyber defense strategies. For instance, the European Network and Information Security Agency (ENISA) held a cyber security exercise in October 2014, involving 29 countries and more than 200 organizations. This included government bodies, telecoms companies, energy suppliers, financial institutions and Internet service providers.

Other sensible precautions can be taken by organizations to minimize losses from cyber criminals. With proper levels of preparation and specialist assistance, it is possible to control damages, as well as recover from a cyber breach and its consequences. Due to growth and impact of social media and other technological innovations, we live in an increasingly networked world, from personal banking to government infrastructure. Cyber threats constantly take aim at secret, political, military, or infrastructural assets of a nation, or its people. Therefore, cybersecurity is a critical part of any governments' security strategy; protecting these networks is paramount.

A combination of technical factors, increased human activity, and notable events such as our recent presidential election, have provided a critical moment in efforts for cybersecurity. The field is growing rapidly in importance due to increasing reliance on computer systems and the Internet in most societies, wireless networks (i.e. Bluetooth and Wi-Fi), and the growth of "smart" devices (smartphones, televisions, tablets, etc.) To secure a computer system, it is important to understand the attacks that can be made against it, and these threats can be classified into numerous categories.

Ransomware has surpassed other cyber-threats in terms of impact. Global campaigns indiscriminately affect victims across various industries in the public and private sectors. There have been specific attacks against critical national infrastructures, which could endanger lives. Poor connectivity and security practices can allow such a threat to rapidly spread and expand.

Payment fraud affects practically every industry, namely the retail, airline and accommodation sectors. Several sectors are targeted by fraudsters, because the services they provide can be used to facilitate other crimes. Such offenses include human or drug trafficking and illegal immigration.

Attacks on bank networks manipulate card balances, take over ATMs, and directly transfer funds. The latter is known as payment process compromise, which is one of the serious emerging threats in this area.

Chapter 2
Defining Cybersecurity

Section Topics

❖ **Areas of Focus**

❖ **Getting Started**

❖ **Statistics**

❖ **Setting Up a Cybersecurity Network**

Areas of Focus

There are three major areas of focus for modern cybersecurity intelligence. Cybersecurity is often discussed inside boardrooms and among front-line employees; however, the concept of cybersecurity is more nuanced than many realize. With various developments coming from criminals, professional hackers, and those defending sensitive data, it can be complex to gain a comprehensive understanding of cybersecurity. Business leaders have to concern themselves with understanding changes in the field and whatever steps they can take to ensure continuity of security efforts despite advances. However, cyber security efforts are not merely confined to the corporate world. There are innumerable political, social, and personal factors involving numerous actors that perform these actions. These are some of the possible motivating factors, as well as potential actors involved in cyber warfare.

Possible Motivating Factors:

> Espionage
> Fraud
> War
> Social/political messages
> Recruitment

Potential Actors:

> Nation-states
> Dictators
> Hacktivists
> Organized Criminals
> Insiders

Identifying major areas of focus can help with directing time and resources to the appropriate areas in the cybersecurity world. Furthermore, a communal approach to cybersecurity broadens awareness and reduces the chances that the same attack could prove successful at companies that share commonalities. Each of these areas will be covered more in depth in Chapter 3.

Many companies focus on internal improvements when it comes to cybersecurity, but often it is not sufficient for complete awareness and protection. Organizations must have a certain level of contact with other businesses inside and outside of their industries and markets. The Obama administration worked with various industry groups to push for increased information sharing and communal awareness to combat cyberattacks. For example, breaches and attempts in the automotive industry (due in part to increased connectivity of cars) have led to an alliance among major auto manufacturers.

Cars and other forms of transportation have increasingly incorporated computer systems to help with areas such as safety and navigation. Therefore, cybersecurity is among the industry's top priorities, and the auto industry is continuously working to enhance vehicle security features. Vehicles have built-in security features that help to protect safety, auto control systems, and other important systems. These tools are isolated from communications-based functions such as navigation and satellite radio. Additionally, software updates require special codes.

Getting Started

The ways of enacting cybersecurity solutions include communicating with others about emerging threats. The NC4 Mission Center Cyber Threat Exchange allows companies to discuss potential problems quickly and carefully, while simultaneously staying informed. It also helps with planning coordinated responses that are often significantly more effective than individual efforts. With a high level of control over the data shared, NC4 Mission Center Cyber Threat Exchange and its components serves a high-performing solution for a wide variety of companies, as well as domestic and foreign government agencies.

The following model is for the NC4 Cyber Threat Exchange Components, via YouTube. This explains how cyber threat intelligence and cybersecurity awareness is exchanged and shared.

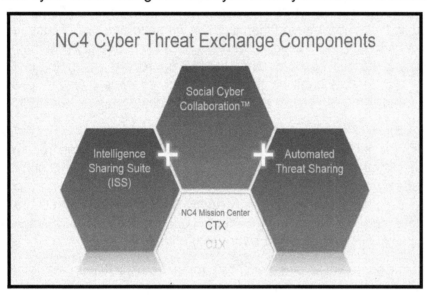

Years (actually decades) of effort and billions of dollars are spent annually to protect digital assets. In recent times, however, on almost a weekly basis, there is news of major cyber security breaches. These major breaches are often devastating in terms of lost revenue, stock price decline, negative press, damage to reputation, lawsuits, internal investigations, and the distractions caused to the business and/or people involved. For instance, it has been widely suggested that cyber breaches by WikiLeaks during the 2016 primaries and general election strongly influenced the decision-making of voters. Therefore, cyber risk has been at or near the top of board and audit committee agendas. Audit committees have to be informed by a knowledgeable Chief Information Security Officer or Chief Information Officer, with four key areas of focus:

- ❖ Periodically review management's cyber security risk assessment

- ❖ Understand the company's cyber security strategy and governance structure

- ❖ Insist on a cyber security scorecard

- ❖ Understand the company's cyber-incident response plan

These four topics will be covered in depth in   Chapter 4.

Statistics

Analyst reports, vendor surveys, and research studies offer a wealth of important statistics on the current state of cybersecurity within industries and the government. Statistics are important because organizations get a sense of emerging threats and how their security controls and processes compare against established practices and trends of the industry. Statistics help to form topics and discussions that help to shape cybersecurity at the enterprise and government levels.

There are statistics that are staggering and too many of them can be frightening; involving cyber crimes and data breaches over the last 2 years. Over 169 million personal records were exposed in 2015, which stemmed from 781 publicized breaches across the financial, business, education, as well as government and healthcare industries. Furthermore, in 2015, there were 38 percent more security incidents detected than in 2014. The average global cost per each lost or stolen record with confidential and sensitive data was $154. The industry with the highest cost per stolen record was the healthcare industry, at $363 per record. According to IBM X-Force data, as of July 31st 2016, 200 million government records worldwide were already compromised. That's nearly 60 million more than the records compromised from 2013 through 2015 combined.

The Internet Crime Complaint Center (IC3) Web site issues a list of complaints received from January 1 to December 31 on any given year covering many different fraud and non-fraud categories. They include auction fraud, non-delivery of merchandise, credit card fraud, computer intrusions, spam/unsolicited email, and child pornography. All of these complaints are accessible to local, state, and federal law enforcement in order to support active investigations, trend analysis, as well as public outreach and awareness efforts.

Here is the Top 10 Most Common IC3 Complaint Categories from 2009, containing the percent of total complaints received:

2009 Top 10 Most Common IC3 Complaint Categories (Percent of Total Complaints Received)

16.6% FBI Scams

11.9% Non-Delivery Merchandise/Payment

9.8% Advanced Fee Fraud

8.2% Identity Theft

7.3% Overpayment Fraud

6.3% Miscellaneous Frauds

6.2% Spam

6.0% Credit Card Fraud

5.7% Auction Fraud

4.5% Computer Damage

2015 Top 10 Most Common IC3 Complaint Categories

Non-Payment/Non-Delivery 67,375

419/Overpayment 30,855

Identity Theft 21,949

Auction 21,510

Other 19,963 IPR

Personal Data Breach 19,632

Employment 18,758

Extortion 17,804

Credit Card Fraud 17,172

Phishing/Vishing/Smishing/Pharming 16,594

Here are the 2015 categories, now adjusted to the amount of complaints received:

United States 80.2%
United Kingdom 2.47%
Nigeria 2.2%
China 1.91%
India 1.46%

Here are the top 5 countries of cybercrime perpetrators around the world, and how it has changed in seven years.

Top 5, 2009 Countries by Count: Perpetrators (Numbered by Rank)

United States 65.4%
United Kingdom 9.9%
Nigeria 8.0%
Canada 2.6%
Malaysia 0.7%

By 2015, the United States was still ranked number 1, but the percentage increased significantly, while other perpetrators in other countries decreased.

Top 5 2015 Countries by Count: Perpetrators (Numbered by Rank)

The cybersecurity industry is growing with more specialists joining the ranks. This is necessary to combat the increasing number of malware that launches daily (approximately 230,000 new malware samples are developed each day). Consequently, more resources are being deployed to counter cyber attacks; with the estimated annual cost for cyber crime committed globally totaling $100 billion. That money is accrued from hackers targeting corporations, banks or celebrities, as well as individual users. The total annualized cost of cyber crime in 2015 in ranged from a low of $0.31 million to a high of $65 million.

Caution

Anyone that is connected to the Internet can be affected by cyber crime, and it can be underestimated how dangerous it is to go online without proper protection. On FBI's Most Wanted List for cyber criminals, 19 individuals have been responsible for consumer losses ranging from $350,000 to over $100 million. They are from various parts of the world and huge rewards are offered for their capture.

Source: https://www.fbi.gov/wanted/cyber

Vulnerability

Vulnerability describes a system's susceptibility or weakness that provides attackers with access to the flaw, and the ability to exploit it. These security risks lead to confusion and the potential for significant loss. Multiple working and fully implemented attacks are described as exploitable vulnerabilities.

Approximately 59% of organizations have experienced a malware infiltration over a period of six months, and during that period of time, 19% of organizations are said to have not conducted security testing. Additionally, 30% of organizations have been successfully attacked with ransomware over the past year or so. The importance of security testing has significantly increased for organizations, with the majority of them considering security vulnerability testing to be a best practice.

A security risk can be classified as vulnerability, leading to confusion. The risk is tied to the potential of a significant loss. There are also vulnerabilities without risk, such as an affected asset without any value. A vulnerability with one or more instances of fully implemented attacks is called an exploitable vulnerability.

Security bugs (or security defects) are vulnerabilities that are not related to software: For instance, hardware, site, personnel involvement fall into this category. Additionally, programming languages that are difficult to be used effectively can be considered a large source of vulnerabilities.

A resource, whether physical or logical, can contain one or more vulnerabilities that are able to be exploited by threat agents. This often results in compromising of the confidentiality, integrity and availability of resources. These resources belong to an organization and/or other parties involved (customers, suppliers, stakeholders, etc.).

Attacks become active when there are attempts to alter system resources or affect their operations. Passive attacks attempt to learn or make use of system information, but system resources are not affected. Confidentiality is compromised.

Setting Up a Cybersecurity Network

There are various cybersecurity networks around the world that are involved with bringing people into the industry, as well as sharing information and helping users and employees protect themselves.

For instance, the Cyber Security Network (CyberSN), headquartered in Boston, is a cybersecurity staffing company that specializes in permanent and contract staffing for all cybersecurity positions, including cyber security sales positions. CyberSN utilizes various tools and strategies to dramatically decrease the frustration, time and cost associated with job searching for cybersecurity professionals.

Source: cybersn.com

CyberSN provides cyber security staffing services and provides an online training program with detailed training on the skills of security operations. Important areas are covered such as healthcare and benefits management, software development, medical technology, financial, asset management, insurance, etc. The company functions as a technology platform to simplify information needed to acquire qualified professionals and significantly lowering the cost of talent acquisition.

The North Carolina Technology Association provides its members with the opportunity to discuss cybersecurity-related issues. They are also able to share information and the best practices for protecting networks, computers, programs and data.

Source: nctechnology.org

Overseas, there is an Australian Cyber Security Network, which emphasizes innovation, communication and collaboration on cybersecurity. The company's approach is to bring together various stakeholders to engage in real conversations. There is interaction with universities, associations, large and small businesses, cybersecurity innovators, and government entities.

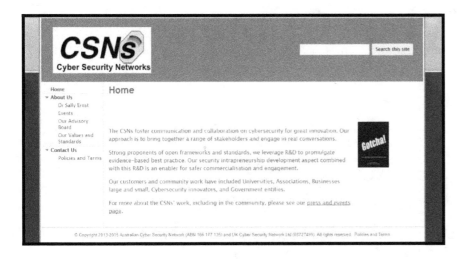

Source: csns.co

Chapter 3
Cyber Crimes

Section Topics

❖ **Cybercrime**

❖ **Phishing**

❖ **Social Engineering**

❖ **Identity Theft**

❖ **Grayware**

Cybercrime

Cybercrime, also called computer crime, is any illegal activity that involves a computer or network-connected device. Cybercrime can be defined concisely as any crime that is committed using a computer network or hardware device. It is the process of using a computer or the internet to commit an illegal act.

The computer or device is capable of being the agent, facilitator, or target of the crime. Perpetrators use the Internet to commit traditional crimes, with a blend of cyber and non-cyber activities. Consequently, there are potential mass casualty attacks or attacks on critical infrastructure. For instance, the perpetrator of the July 2012 shooting in an Aurora, CO movie theater used the Internet to purchase and stockpile the weapons, ammunition, and protective equipment.

Cybercrimes are a domestic and international problem committed anywhere around the world due to the development of new technologies. It has now surpassed illegal drug trafficking as a criminal moneymaker; an identity is stolen every 3 seconds due to cybercrime. Cybercrimes hurt small businesses in particular, as 60 percent of the businesses targeted in those attacks go out of business within six months. They are at a disadvantage, due to a lack of resources to respond to the cybercrimes, or the capital to absorb the losses. And that isn't always because of the loss of money. But data is often the more important target than money, as people steal information and intellectual property, as well as consumer data. Cybercrime is a bigger risk now than ever before due to the sheer number of connected people and devices.

When a user downloads a program, there is always a risk, because the code may contain a virus, Trojan horse, and other malicious codes. Furthermore, without a sophisticated security package, a PC can become infected within four minutes of connecting to the Internet.

Cyber attacks on social media are frequent because social media users usually trust their circles of online friends. Consequently, over 600,000 Facebook accounts are compromised every single day! Also, 1 in 10 social media users said they've been a victim of a cyber attack, with numbers on the rise.

Phishing

Phishing is described as email messages, websites, and phone calls designed to steal money and important information. Phishing is a form of fraud in which there are attempts to obtain information such as login credentials or account information by masquerading as a reputable individual in various communication channels. Cybercriminals are able do this by installing malicious software or stealing personal information off of computers. Typically a victim receives a message that appears to have been sent by a known contact or organization. An attachment or links in the message can install malware on the user's device or direct them to a malicious website where they divulge personal and financial information (passwords, account IDs or credit card, social security numbers, etc.).

The reason that phishing is popular with cybercriminals, is that it is far easier to trick someone into clicking a malicious link in a seemingly legitimate email than attempting to break through a computer's security defenses. Popular websites or companies are spoofed, which refers to scam artists using graphics in emails or texts that appear to be connected to legitimate websites. Cybercriminals also use web addresses that resemble the names of well-known companies, but in actuality, they are slightly altered. Though some phishing emails are poorly written and clearly fake, sophisticated cybercriminals employ techniques to create effective types of messages, known as phishing "hooks". They get the highest open or click-through rate and Facebook posts that generate the most likes. Phishing campaigns commonly occur around the year's major events and holidays. They take advantage of breaking news stories, both true and fictitious.

Phishing messages look like they are genuinely from a well-known company, containing logos and other identifying information stolen directly from that company's website. The malicious links within the body of the message are designed to make it appear that they go to the spoofed organization. Users don't often pay attention to misspelled URLs (typosquatting), and URLs created using different logical characters to read exactly like a trusted domain (homograph spoofing). Here is an example, with a spoofed version of Amazon, with all the identifiable graphics, headings, and links. However, if you look on the URL, you will notice "amazon.com". Such a website does not exist.

Source: my.graceland.edu/ICS/icsfs/notamazon.jpg?target=d4951daa-9894-4a79-b685-abc45795ce6b

ITunes users are phishing targets, with fake iTunes emails disguised as invoices. Scammers spoof the look and feel of iTunes communications, to make it look like an official statement. The email "claims that you have been overcharged for a download purchase — $25 for one song, which is usually $1.99 or less, or $45 for the Netflix app." Scammers want users to click on the link to manage their account and receive their refund. By clicking on the link, malware may download onto the computer or smartphone, or you may be taken to a website asking you to provide personal information that could be used in identity theft.

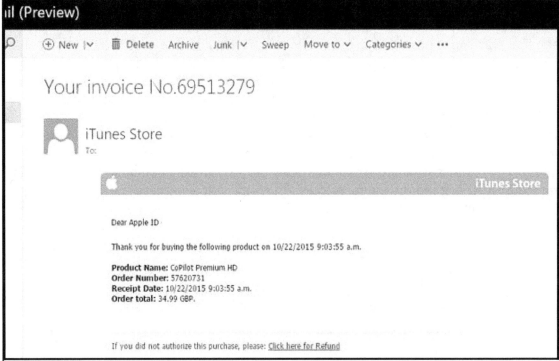

Source:

i.telegraph.co.uk/multimedia/archive/03480/appleinvoice_3480998b.jpg

Social Engineering

Social engineering is the psychological manipulation of people into performing actions and/or divulging important confidential information, and gaining system access. It is a type of con that it is often one of many steps involved in a more complex fraud scheme. The term "social engineering" is an act of psychological manipulation also associated with the social sciences, but has gained increasing prominence overtime among computer and information security professionals. Social engineering occurs through many forms, but some of the most common techniques used by fraudsters include invoice fraud, the aforementioned phishing, vishing, and social media.

Invoice Fraud

Fraudsters also send emails that appear to be legitimate, but are intended to trick the recipient into disclosing sensitive information. For example, there is invoice fraud, where criminals send a phishing email to the supplier asking for confirmation of the invoice payment date and amount due. The supplier unknowingly confirms, thinking that he or she is communicating with the "customer". Invoice fraud occurs when a fraudster attempts to impersonate a supplier, whose invoice is due for payment, appearing to know various details (by hacking into accounts) regarding the invoice that is due for payment such as the payment date. The fraudsters then use those details for credibility, in their attempt to impersonate the supplier when contacting the customer company. The company issuing the invoice can lower its guard, and the fraudster then provides the company with the "new" bank account details for the payment. That individual disappears when the payment is made, with money rapidly withdrawn or dispersed through various accounts. Invoice fraudsters can impersonate the supplier via telephone or by using a spoof email address purportedly originating from the supplier. Banks, accountants and solicitors commonly fall victim to invoice fraud. There are some phishing emails that appear authentic, but there are also unsophisticated phishing emails that contain obvious errors and mistakes. That alone should raise red flags to recipients of the email. This is a result of being created by some fraudsters who do not speak English as a first language.

Vishing

Vishing or "vocal phishing" is the same as phishing, but this occurs over the phone, and sometimes can be more successful. Vishing preys on the victim's human nature in terms of being reluctant to reject a seemingly innocent request for information. Vishing attempts involve impersonating supply chain management, a company CEO, the police or other authority figures, utility providers, delivery companies, and other important professions and occupations. The perpetrators create a sense of trust combined with urgency, and the user feels pressured into making an immediate decision. As with email addresses and URLs, caller ID details can be spoofed to trick recipients into thinking they are speaking to someone in particular. For example, cybercriminals may call to offer to help solve your computer problems or sell you a software license. It should be noted that Microsoft DOES NOT make unsolicited phone calls (cold calls) to charge for computer security or software fixes. Additionally, cybercriminals might inquire about your user name and password or ask you to go to a website to install software that allows access to your computer. This potentially compromises the computer system and personal information.

Social Media

Cyber attackers have an affinity for social media, because users that spend a lot of time on social networks are very likely to click links posted by trusted friends. Hackers use this to their advantage. Here are some common types of attacks:

❖ **Like-jacking**: Occurs when criminals post fake Facebook "like" buttons to web pages. Users who click the button don't actually "like" the page, but instead download malware.

❖ **Link-jacking**: A practice used to redirect one website's links to another which hackers use to redirect users from trusted websites to malware infected websites.

❖ **Social spam**: Unwanted spam content appearing on social networks and any website with user-generated content (comments, chat, etc.). Social spam appears through messages, profanity, insults, hate speech, malicious links, fraudulent reviews, fake friends, and personally identifiable information.

Identity Theft

Identity theft is defined as the stealing of personal information that enables cyber criminals to impersonate someone else. Cyber criminals steal identity through a simple email address where the cybercriminal will send you a phishing email that lures you to a phishing site. This is where more personal information is entered, such as your name, bank account or credit card details. When more personal information is collected, the victim becomes more susceptible to their money being stolen. For instance, the 2016 Identity Fraud Study, released by Javelin Strategy & Research, found that $15 billion was stolen from 13.1 million U.S. consumers in 2015. Additionally, identity thieves have stolen $112 billion in the previous six years. The stolen personal information can for online shopping, opening bank accounts, and borrowing and transferring money out of a compromised bank account.

Cybercriminals can pick up personal information by researching the victim online (e.g. visiting their Facebook, LinkedIn, and Google searching for background info). If the cybercriminal has infiltrated the victim's PC with malware, they can obtain user names and passwords, credit card numbers, date of birth, etc. This is valuable information that can enable cybercriminals to succeed in impersonating the victim online. They can drain the victim's bank account of money, use his or her personal credit card, obtain a fraudulent identity card, and commit various other criminal acts.

A hacker dubbed "The Collector" claimed to be behind one of the largest security and email breaches in recent history. This breach affected nearly every individual with an email account, including Gmail, Microsoft Outlook (or Hotmail), Yahoo Mail and many others. Approximately 273 million email accounts were posted for sale online, and cybersecurity experts estimate that The Collector has possession of up to 1.7 billion email account passwords.

Furthermore, there is confirmation by Yahoo of a massive breach of their customers' data, which exposed over 500 million Yahoo accounts and affected Yahoo services. The information stolen may include names, email addresses, telephone numbers, birthdays, passwords and security questions and answers. Yahoo believes that a "state-sponsored actor" was behind the attack, which implies that a foreign government was responsible for the data breach.

Grayware

Grayware is potentially unwanted or misleading applications that often are bundled with installers for other applications. Grayware (or greyware) is a general term that describes applications that behave in a manner that is annoying or undesirable, such as spyware, adware, remote access tools, and any other unwelcome files and programs. These files and programs are designed to harm the performance of computers on your network. The term grayware has been in use since at least September 2004, and is also referred to as potentially unwanted programs (PUPs).

Grayware is applications or files that are not classified as viruses or Trojan horse programs, but can have a similar adverse effect on system performance and security.

For instance, the thousands of add-ons available for Mozilla Firefox and Chrome act like normal applications, with links established with cloud servers collecting user information and activity trends.

Often grayware performs a variety of annoying actions such as irritating users with pop-up windows and tracking user habits and behaviors.

 Smartphones and tablets are also increasingly at risk of picking up grayware, due to the prevalence of installing mobile apps (short for applications), often with little thought of the potential to access and use our personal information. When cloud servers are compromised or infected, malware gets a backdoor right into countless corporate networks. Conventional anti-virus software and firewalls become ineffective in minimizing vulnerability. Security applications can differentiate between "white" (safe) and "black" (malicious) software, but the "grays" are often difficult to decipher. The two most common types of grayware are adware and spyware.

33

Adware

Adware's primary objective is to make money via advertising. The target audience is you, the computer or mobile device user. Personal data can be collected and sent to a third party. Adware utilizes that information to display ads tailored to a particular profile. Users could inadvertently agree to install bundled adware and spyware through end-user license agreements on free software. There are also seemingly legitimate pop-up windows offering a free antivirus scan, a prize or a software update that can spread adware.

Opening links or attachments in compromised emails, texts or app messages also can bring adware. In addition to security concerns, both adware and spyware disk space consume memory and processing resources, which may slow your computer down.

Spyware

Spyware is a blanket term given to software whose main objective is to track and record online behavior, and submit this information to a third party, typically for marketing purposes. This information can include confidential, financial and personal account usernames and passwords, in addition to credit card details. Spyware doesn't overtly ask for consent to install components or to use the data it collects from the user and/or the device. It works covertly to avoid detection.

Spyware is usually downloaded along with software such as a video or music file-sharing program. Here is an example of such a potential program, called the Freemake Video Downloader, which I have installed on my computer.

Chapter 4
Government Hacking and Espionage

Section Topics

- ❖ **Government Hacking**
- ❖ **Hacktivism**
- ❖ **Espionage**

Government Hacking

Cyberattacks and breaches have grown in frequency, often with major corporate, political, and monetary consequences. In 2014, the number of U.S. data breaches hit a record 783, with 85.6 million records exposed (not counting Yahoo's 2014 breach of over 500 million users). The number of breaches in 2015 was virtually the same at 781, and the number of records exposed doubled to about 169 million. In 2015, the majority of data breaches affected medical/healthcare organizations (66.7 percent of total breaches) and government/military (20.2 percent), according to the Identity Theft Resource Center. However, these figures do not include the many attacks that go unreported and/or undetected.

The U.S. government has also been the target of hackers. Breaches at the Federal Deposit Insurance Corp. and the Internal Revenue Service follow multiple breaches in May 2015 of the Office of Personnel Management and the Department of the Interior where the records of 22 million current and former U.S. government employees were compromised. In June 2016, 154 million voters had private information stolen in a massive breach, and earlier that same year, a database with around 191 million voter records was hacked and released online. For the latter, the stolen information included names, addresses, party affiliation, phone numbers and voting history. A following breach compromised the records for 54 million voters. In November 2015, a hacking organization known as Crackas with Attitude (CWA) allegedly was behind the hack against then-CIA Director John Brennan's personal email, and managed to breach a digital portal used by the FBI and other law enforcement agencies throughout the U.S. This portal stored arrest records, data about active shooters and terrorists and a real-time messaging system controlled by law enforcement agencies. The hackers leaked some of the stolen data, including the contact information of some government employees and local law enforcement agents. Both intelligence and law enforcement officials agree that there is a mountain of circumstantial evidence suggesting that the Russia was behind the hacking of the Democratic National Committee, and furthermore, was primarily aimed at helping presidential candidate Donald Trump damage and smear his opponent, Hillary Clinton. American intelligence officials believe that Russia also penetrated databases housing Republican National Committee data, but only chose to release documents concerning the Democratic Party.

It was announced in January 2017 that a "statelike actor" infiltrated the Czech Foreign Ministry and hacked emails belonging to the foreign minister and dozens of his colleagues, quite reminiscent of the breach of the Democratic National Committee's servers. The announcement immediately raised fears across Central Europe of potential interference by Russia. Legislative elections are expected to be held in October, which is another unnerving resemblance to the DNC hack. This repeated attack was detected only during a recent systems check, according to officials. Experts agreed that the government had likely downplayed the scope of the attack. Highly sensitive messages were reportedly downloaded, in what is described as one of the most serious breaches in years.

In March of the same year, WikiLeaks released a trove of documents detailing the CIA's capacity to hack numerous devices, which sent major tech companies into scrambling mode. They have been forced to attempt to rapidly increase information sharing in order to protect users from prying eyes. Though there are few specifics, there are enough technical details for security experts and product vendors to recognize widespread compromises exist as a result of these leaks. Dozens of firms rushed to contain the damage from possible security weak points following WikiLeaks' claims. For instance, Sinan Eren, vice president of Czech anti-virus software maker Avast (named by WikiLeaks as a target of the CIA), called on Apple and Google to supply security firms with privileged access to their devices to offer immediate fixes to known bugs. WikiLeaks describes these leaks as the biggest in the Central Intelligence Agency's history.

Hacktivism

Hacktivism is the main motivation that drives cyber attacks, accounting for half of them worldwide. The term represents a rebellious use of computers and computer networks in order to promote a political agenda. It contains roots in hacker culture and ethics, often related to free speech, human rights, or freedom of information. Hacktivism emerged in the late 1980s, when hacking for fun and profit emerged as noticeable threats, and initially it took the form of computer viruses and worms that spread messages of protest. One of the most notable examples of early hacktivism is "Worms Against Nuclear Killers (WANK)," a computer worm that Australian anti-nuclear activists unleashed into the networks of the NASA and the US Department of Energy in 1989. This was done to protest the launch of a shuttle carrying radioactive plutonium. Hacktivism can be based on politically-motivated technology hacking, anarchic civil disobedience, or an undefined anti-systemic gesture.

Anti-spam activists, security experts, or open source advocates are also capable of having involvement in hacktivism.

2016 was the year hacktivists disrupted cyberspace like never before. The top cyber trend in 2016 was hacktivism, with state and local governments being targeted. There was also the emergence of fake news, leaked insider information to the press, and claims and counterclaims by public officials. This resulted in a covert undermining of news media and government source authority, credibility, trust and legitimacy.

New technologies provided protesters with a convenient and powerful means to spread messages and mobilize globally. Additionally, technological innovations gave protesters the ability to employ hacking tools to conduct cyber operations analogous to street protests and sit-ins.

Anonymous is likely most widely known hacktivist group in the world, with related offshoots and regional and local affiliates responsible for thousands of cyber-attacks worldwide. They have breached governments, companies, churches, terrorists, drug dealers, and pedophiles, while also working with other hacktivists in large-scale operations.

Espionage

Cyber espionage has clearly evolved since the pre-Internet days of the Cold War. It is not the electronic equivalent of overhearing a conversation, but more like breaking into a neighbor's home. It involves actively breaking into an adversary's computer network and installing malicious software that takes over the network. Cyber espionage is a form of attacks that violates the sovereignty of another country, causing considerable diplomatic and geopolitical costs.

Espionage is the act or practice of obtaining secrets without the permission of the holder of the information. It is illegal obtaining of information considered secret or confidential. This information is typically of personal, sensitive, proprietary or classified nature. The spying occurs with individuals, competitors, rivals, groups, governments and enemies in order to gain a personal, economic, political or military advantage. With cyber espionage, various methods are employed via networks or individual computers by utilizing cracking techniques and malicious software, including Trojan horses and spyware. Espionages can be perpetrated online from computer desks of professionals based in other countries or may involve infiltration at home by computer-trained spies and moles. It also may simply be amateur malicious hackers and software programmers. Espionage is often part of an institutional effort by a government or commercial concern, in addition to state spying on potential or actual enemies primarily for military purposes. Cyber espionage typically involves the use of access to secrets and classified information or control of individual computers or whole networks. This is done for a strategic advantage and for psychological and political activities and/or sabotage. It also involves analysis of public activity on social networking sites like Facebook and Twitter.

Hacking is considered to be the new face of espionage. It is not just simply undercover agents trying to recruit a mole or cracking safes to steal sensitive information; nowadays the battle is fought with keyboards and software. U.S. intelligence officials have stated that Russian-based hacking unit APT29 (or Cozy Bear) has sent out a barrage of emails with a malicious link to thousands of recipients, including the U.S. government. Once the link is clicked, hackers can access the system. The hackers have been implicated in the D.N.C. breach of the 2016 elections, beginning as early as the summer of 2015. A document states that this group "successfully compromised" the "U.S. political party" and stole "email from several accounts." A malicious activity code has been unleashed named Grizzly Steppe. American Edward Snowden is one of the most famous examples of espionage in modern times and is largely viewed as either a pariah or martyr, depending on your political beliefs and ideologies. The former National Security Agency contractor leaked documents about top-secret surveillance programs, resulting in a charge by the U.S. government of three felonies, including two under the Espionage Act (the 1917 statute enacted to criminalize dissent against World War I

Chapter 5
Enforcement of

Cybersecurity

Section Topics

❖ **Examples of Enacting Cybersecurity**

❖ **Challenges of Enacting Cybersecurity**

❖ **Ways of Enacting Cybersecurity**

❖ **Examples of Enacting Cybersecurity**

Examples of Enacting Cybersecurity

Cyber threats have enormous implications for government security, economic prosperity, and personal and public safety. States and countries are addressing cybersecurity through various robust approaches. They include requiring government or public agencies to implement security practices, offering incentives to the cybersecurity industry, creating cybersecurity commissions, studies or task forces promoting cybersecurity training and education, and capturing and prosecuting cyber perpetrators.

New York

On March 1, 2017, the state of New York has passed the nation's first cybersecurity regulations designed to protect consumers, in addition to ensuring the security of the state's financial services industry. New York is the first to pursue this initiative. Other financial institutions across the nation should expect similar regulations due to amount of increasing cyber-attacks.

The new regulations require several guidelines that institutions must adhere to, including drafting a written cybersecurity policy, appointing a Chief Information Security Officer, implementing an audit trail system, reviewing access privileges, requirement of multi-factor authentication and cybersecurity awareness training, and the maintenance of data related to cybersecurity events for three years.

DefenseStorm

DefenseStorm is a company that urges financial institutions to take a more hands-on approach to cybersecurity to not only stay ahead of bad actors, and impending regulations for other states as well. Sean Feeney, the CEO of DefenseStorm believes that the regulations will have a domino effect on other states, with the rise in high-profile security breaches.

Source:https://www.defensestorm.com/

Cost of a Data Breach Study

The economic cost of being hacked is quite substantial. According to the Ponemon Institute's 2016 Cost of a Data Breach Study, the total average organizational cost of a data breach is $7.01 million, while the average cost per record breached is $221. Astonishingly, those numbers continue to rise. The average cost of legal proceedings against perpetrators is $500,000; fines issued by federal authorities can range from $5,000 to $100,000. In addition to these costs, there are also reputational risks that can potentially impact financial institutions. The financial and reputational costs of a data breach, combined with the implementation of new cybersecurity regulations, increases the need for effective cybersecurity.

Idaho Gov. C.L. "Butch" Otter signed an executive order enacting recommendations of a Cybersecurity Task Force to keep the state secure from cyber threats. The recommendations support state agencies in implementing the best cybersecurity practices, as well as addressing the need for employee education and training. The recommendations include developing a public outreach program to share best practices and up-to-date information. Additionally, they include appointing a director of information security to lead efforts to identify and prevent hacks on the State of Idaho's computer networks. The Cybersecurity Task Force was created in July 2015 spearheaded by Lt. Gov. Brad Little, including state agency directors and private sector specialists. The task force worked with business and industry experts and national cybersecurity specialists to develop the recommendations.

China

During the same week that China passed a sweeping new National Security Law, the Chinese government published a draft Cybersecurity Law. The draft law unveiled the government's priorities related to cyberspace and information networks. It also combined existing cybersecurity-related requirements, and granted government agencies more powers with cyberactivity regulations.

Yahoo

In March 2017, four suspects were indicted in a massive hack of Yahoo emails, by a grand jury in California for computer hacking, economic espionage and other criminal offences. Two of them allegedly were officers of the Russian Federal Security Service who allegedly masterminded and directed the hacking, according to the justice department. They allegedly tasked one of the suspect with hacking more than 80 accounts in exchange for commissions. Yahoo sent an email in September 2016 alerting users that their account information (email addresses, telephone numbers, and dates of birth, passwords and security questions) were stolen in a cyber attack two years prior. Yahoo is also facing a proposed $50-million class action lawsuit related to the personal information of Canadian users, in addition to various class actions in the United States.

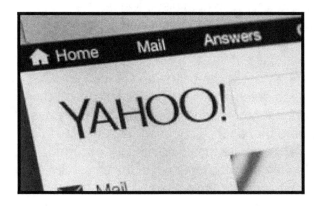

Other

New, high-priority mandates were introduced such as protection of critical information infrastructure and more systematic development of existing legal requirements in areas such as data localization, cross-border data transfer and security reviews. Previously under-regulated or unregulated activities that take place over computer networks will be subject to government scrutiny once the law is fully implemented.

Challenges of Enacting Cybersecurity

Even though the world is more interconnected than ever before, with numerous advantages, increased connectivity brings increased risk of theft, fraud, and abuse. There is increased vulnerability to cyber attacks such as government and corporate security breaches, phishing, and social media fraud. Cybersecurity and law enforcement capabilities are critical to safeguarding and securing cyberspace, as law enforcement performs an essential role in national and international cybersecurity objectives by investigating a wide range of cybercrimes, and apprehending and prosecuting those responsible.

Legislation

Legislation was introduced/considered in at least 28 states in 2016. Fifteen of those states enacted legislation, many addressing issues related to security practices and protection of information in government agencies, exemptions from state, freedom of information or public records acts and cyber/computer crimes. However, there were 46 instances that the law was ruled "failed". It can also be frustrating for the victims when the perpetrators are never truly brought to justice. There are local police departments that have set up divisions specifically devoted to computer crimes enforcement. However, some shy away from investigating and enforcing these types of crime because enforcing laws governing online behavior is naturally more difficult than enforcing traditional laws.

Jurisdiction

Jurisdiction pertains to which agency or court has the authority to administer justice in a particular matter, to the extent of the agencies' and courts' authority. Jurisdiction is based on three broad branches of law: criminal law, civil law, and regulatory law. Before a law enforcement agency can fully investigate a cybercrime case, it has to have proper jurisdiction in order to have enforcement of cybercrime laws. The first thing that must be determined is whether a crime has taken place at all. The next one to determine is the geographic jurisdiction. In terms of geographic jurisdiction, a law enforcement agency or court has jurisdiction only over crimes that take place in the geographic location where that agency or court has authority. This includes the location of the perpetrator, victim, or location where the crime actually occurred. This case is more difficult to determine because often the perpetrator is not in the same city, state or country as the victim. Geographic jurisdiction is further complicated because laws differ in state and nation. An act that's illegal in one location may not be in another. Things become further complicated if the perpetrator is in a location where the action isn't actually against the law, though it's a clear-cut crime in the location where the victim is. Law enforcement agencies can only enforce the law within their jurisdictions. A police officer or FBI agent commissioned in one state has no authority to arrest someone in another state or country. Extradition is difficult at best, and often impossible, as evidenced by the debate with Edward Snowden. Under international law, a country has no obligation to turn over a criminal. Although some countries have treaties agreeing to do so, it can be expensive and a long, drawn-out process.

Anonymity and identity is also crucial, before jurisdiction even comes into play. It is highly necessary to discover where and who the criminal is before an arrest is made. Online crime is particularly problematic because there are so many ways to hide one's identity. Various services will mask a user's IP address by routing traffic through different servers (usually for a fee), thus making difficult to track down the criminal. Additionally, attempts to better track online identity and potentially end anonymity are controversial among privacy advocates and could result in political backlash.

Evidence

Nature of the evidence makes cybercrime more difficult to investigate and prosecute in comparison to other "real world" crimes. Digital evidence is merely a collection of ones and zeros represented by magnetization, light pulses, radio signals, etc. This is fragile and easily changeable information.

Ways of Enacting Cybersecurity

The importance of cybersecurity must be communicated from the top down, from the board of directors to every level of the organization. Each employee needs to have an important responsibility in order to protect the organization, its mission, and ultimately the livelihood of each individual on the team. Effective cybersecurity training can occur either through interactive computer-based delivery or an onsite classroom setting. Training out can be spread throughout the year to reinforce security culture and stay on top of evolving threats. HR department should be equipped with programs that mitigate employee dissatisfaction, because it can lower the risk of malicious insider threats.

It is generally believed that organizations should have a security governance program involving representatives from multiple department, with policies and processes developed, analyzed and enacted. This program does not just pertain to the IT department, but the whole organization's approach in terms of securing data. An organization should also have an incident response and crisis management plan available to enact in the event of a security breach. These theories and opinions culminated in the creation of a "Cybersecurity Bill of Rights," in 2015 by the National Association of Insurance Commissioners (NAIC). This is intended to be used as a model law for insurance companies and agencies. The bill requires firms to draft a privacy policy and post on their website, and then take steps to enact cyber defense. It also provides customers with written notice of a data breach, if the breach occurred within 60 days of discovering it. After some initial criticism, the NAIC revised and republished the bill last month.

It has been argued that Congress could specify what government assistance can help private entities defend against cyber-attacks, as well as determining the confidentiality would be involved. Other than a provision in National Security Directive 42 regarding possible National Security Agency assistance to government contractors, no government agency other than law enforcement is authorized to help a private company. This only allowed when there is a nation state-sponsored attack. No company, including communications providers, has the resources to combat the capabilities of a nation state. Therefore, providing a government-backup capability law to U.S. businesses send a powerful message to countries contemplating attacks. Congress could also provide funding and leadership in advancing effective cybercrime laws in the US, while promoting international assistance in cybercrime investigations. Publicly listed companies can be directed to specify in Securities and Exchange Commission filings whether cybersecurity plan, policies and procedures have fully and effectively been implemented.

Patriot Act

Source: patriotact.com

The USA PATRIOT Act of 2001 established Electronic Crime Task Forces (ECTFs) across the nation. Under the ECTF model, local, state, and federal law enforcement agencies join prosecutors, private-sector companies, and academic experts in order to investigate attacks on the nation's financial and critical infrastructures. These task forces have been said to be the most effective ways to deal with cybercrime, as local agencies provide the on-the ground for the investigations. Additionally, federal agencies can help to connect cases in multiple jurisdictions as well as investigate large-scale operations.

Secret Service

The Secret Service deploys a task force approach through 35 ECTFs that work collaboratively and ensure that all members are aware of every situation encountered through strategic cyber investigations. Some agencies are better equipped for certain types of cases. For over two decades, state and federal governments have passed various statutes to address criminal activities that occurred over the Internet. They include laws against cyberbullying, cyberstalking, theft of wireless services, spamming, and unauthorized access.

Source: wikipedia.org/wiki/United_States_Secret_Service

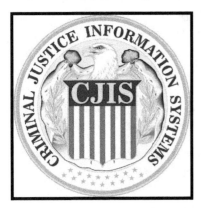

Criminal Justice Information

In 1992, the FBI launched the Criminal Justice Information Services (CJIS), an agency that created a list of compliance codes and best practices that law enforcement entities have to abide by. This agency is vital in protecting critical information. Authentication and encryption are two of the most vital aspects of protecting this data. Authentication serves as a gatekeeper to sensitive data and key systems in order to block and/or track unauthorized access. Encryption prevents hackers from finding a back door in, and gaining access to credentials.

Source: vcitadel.com/experience-world-class-enterprise-security/

Department of Homeland Security

The Department of Homeland Security (DHS) works with other federal agencies to conduct high-impact criminal investigations to disrupt and defeat cyber criminals, prioritize the recruitment and training of technical experts, develop standardized methods, and broadly share cyber response best practices and tools. Criminal investigators and network security experts with deep understanding of the technologies malicious actors are using and the specific vulnerabilities they are targeting work to effectively respond to and investigate cyber incidents.

Source: wikipedia.org/wiki/United_States_Department_of_Homeland_Security

Certificate Authentication

Certificate authentication is vital to improving cybersecurity in law enforcement, because strong digital identities in the form of digital certificates have to be created. This helps agencies zero in on certain devices and stolen date. This form of authentication essentially serves as a passport; anyone who doesn't have this cannot decrypt   the information they access.

Ponemon Institute and IBM Surveys

Cyber risk has to be communicated as an enterprise risk rather than just an IT problem. Budget should be allocated not only for traditional tools and sensors, but for an enterprise-wide approach to security. Organizations are increasingly connected digitally to their customers, suppliers, vendors and the public. Therefore, it is vital that intellectual property, sensitive business information, operational dependencies, company reputation, and customer/patient information must be protected. The latter data has significant value to enterprising cyber criminals. The Ponemon Institute's 2015 Cost of Data Breach study revealed that the healthcare industry has the highest cost per stolen record, at $363. This figure is more than double that of industry averages.

Source: hipaajournal.com/wp-content/uploads/2017/06/ponemon-ibm.jpg

Another disturbing statistic is that an IBM C-Suite survey reported that 60% of Chief Financial Officers (CFOs) and Chief Human Resources Officers (CHROs) believe that they are least engaged in cybersecurity threat management activities, yet distribute much of the heavily coveted data by cybercriminals.

Chapter 6
Ways of Protecting Yourself

Section Topics

❖ Backing Up Data

❖ USB Drives

❖ System Repair Discs (Windows 7 Users)

❖ System Image

❖ Cybersecurity

❖ Passwords and Encryption

Backing up Data

Data is the most important aspect of your computer. An operating system and applications can be reinstalled, but it is difficult or impossible to replicate original data. Computer viruses can bring an abrupt collapse of their computers, while potentially revealing private information. For instance, computer data can include credit card information, passwords, user names, social security numbers, insurance, etc. Additionally, costs for repair or replacement of damaged units can be expensive. Hackers regularly crash operating systems and corrupt/wipe out data through malware, ransomware, and several other viruses. Data can also be destroyed due to system/hardware issues unrelated to hacking (memory, motherboard, CPU fan stops working, etc.), and disasters such as fires, hurricanes, tornados, and flooding. Therefore, files have to be copied over to a protected system that enables access when those files are needed. Users should regularly and repeatedly back up important information, as well as create a plan for recovering from a potential system failure.

USB Drives

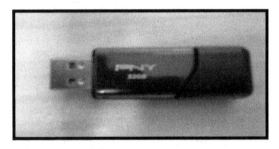

One method for backing up files is use of a USB flash drive. Secure USB flash drives are able to protect the data stored on them from access by unauthorized users. USB flash drive products have been on the market since 2000, and their use and demand has increased exponentially by both consumers and businesses. Because of this, manufacturers are producing faster devices with greater data storage capacities. The files that can be backed up include videos, photos, documents, and software programs.

The above image is a PNY flash drive that I have, containing 32 GB of space. USB flash drives manufactured by PNY come in various storage capacities, which make them ideal for saving large and/or small files.

In order to save files onto a USB drive, insert drive into any available USB slot located on your desktop PC below the DVD/CD drive.

Upon inserting the USB Drive, you may encounter a window asking whether to scan and fix the drive, or to continue without scanning. You can select the latter, but it is also recommended to scan and fix the drive to avoid future problems.

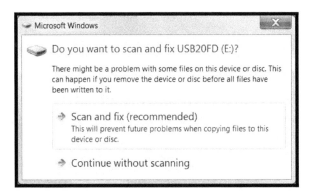

Windows is configured to auto-run it, therefore, you may see this screen pop-up.

Alternatively, if the computer does not auto-run the USB drive, it can be accessed via My Computer.

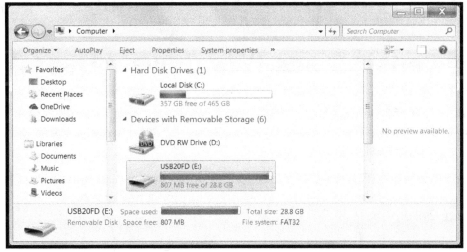

To save whatever application you are using, click File --> Save As...

....then click on the My Computer icon on the left side of the window, then double-click on the USB drive.

Another option is opening the flash drive in a separate window, selecting the file, pressing the left-click button on your mouse, and dragging it to the flash drive location.

One drawback of using USB flash drives is that companies are at risk when sensitive data are stored on unsecured USB flash drives by employees who may use the devices for data outside of the office. The consequences of losing drives loaded with such important information can dire. There is risk of losing customer data, financial information, business plans and other confidential information, along with the associated risk of reputation damage.

System Repair Discs (Windows 7 Users)

For Windows 7 users, if a serious error occurs, you might need to start or boot your computer using the Windows 7 installation disc or a USB flash drive. If your computer won't start Windows at all, you can access Startup Repair in the System Recovery Options menu from the Windows 7 installation disc or USB flash drive.

NOTE: If your computer is a Tablet PC or has a touchscreen, you might need to attach a keyboard and mouse to that device in order to access Startup Repair and other tools in the System Recovery Options menu.

To start Windows 7 from an installation disc or USB flash drive:

1. Turn on the computer
2. Insert the Windows 7 installation disc or USB flash drive, and then turn off your computer.
3. Restart the computer.
4. Press any key when prompted to do so (and follow any subsequent instructions)
5. Click Install now to begin the installation process, at the Install Windows page,

NOTE: You can click on Repair your computer to access system recovery options.

System recovery options help users to repair Windows if a serious error occurs. In order to use the system recovery options, you'll need a Windows installation disc or access to the recovery options. If neither is available, you can create a system repair disc to access the system recovery options.

System Image

A system image is a defined as a copy of the entire state of a computer system, stored in a non-volatile form such as a file. It contains everything on a PC's hard drive, copying everything bit by bit. An image allows the PC to be shut down and restored later to exactly the same state; thus, it can be used for backup. System images can be copied back onto a drive in order to restore the system state. They contain a snapshot of the computer's hard drive at any given time, and equal the approximate amount of space used on a drive. Here is an illustration of how system images can be done in Windows:

1. Click on Start, and go to the Control Panel

2. Click on Backup and Restore

3. Scroll to left side, and click **Create a system image**

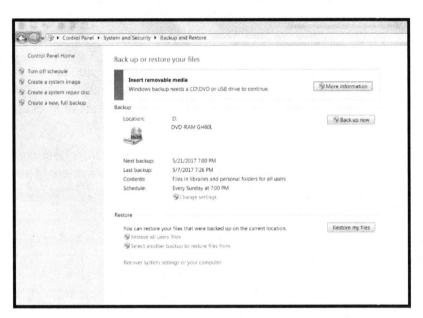

It should be noted that system images are actually not the ideal way to create normal backups of your computer and its files. System images are very large, and often they contain meaningless and/or useless data, such as system files. The ideal method is reinstalling the Windows operating system. Furthermore, in terms of program files, if your hard drive crashes, you can just reinstall these programs on a new Windows system.

Cybersecurity Programs

Computer security software or cybersecurity software is any computer program that helps to enhance information security. Cybersecurity programs enhance the defense of computers against intrusion and unauthorized use of resources. Examples of cybersecurity programs include access control, anti-keyloggers, anti-malware, anti-spyware, antivirus software, firewalls, Intrusion detection system (IDS), and Intrusion prevention system (IPS).

Here is a list of commonly used cybersecurity programs today:

- ❖ McAfee AntiVirus Plus
- ❖ Kaspersky Anti-Virus
- ❖ Bitdefender Antivirus Plus 2016
- ❖ Trend Micro Antivirus + Security
- ❖ Emsisoft Anti-Malware
- ❖ Malwarebytes Anti-Exploit Premium
- ❖ Valt.X Cyber Security for WindowsNorton Security 2017

Companies must have a variety of cyberweapons at their disposal to combat everything ranging from denial-of-service attacks (which overwhelm a website with data requests); to sophisticated malware that exploits previously unknown software flaws. However, with numerous tools and technologies to manage, the administration and coordination can be a nightmare, particularly for larger organizations. An effective approach that organizations should use includes innovative security technologies, world-renowned expertise, and deep threat intelligence capabilities. Furthermore, the entire security operations lifecycle should be addressed, including every critical issue before, during and after an attack.

In 2013, Cisco Systems acquired Sourcefire, a company specializing in network security technology, for $2.7 billion. The acquisition included an intrusion prevention system. The following year, FireEye purchased Mandiant for approximately $1 billion; the former company's strength is in detection, while the latter's expertise is forensics.

A U.S. military agency is researching a plan to move past the software "patch and pray" technique and develop a system that actually stops viruses and hack attacks, rather than gullible hardware that can be tricked and manipulated by software. It is called the System Security Integrated Through Hardware and Firmware program under development by the Defense Advanced Research Projects Agency (DARPA).

Passwords and Encryption

A long and complex online password is a necessary part of proper encryption security. Passwords should contain a random mix of upper case and lower case letters, numbers and symbols. A weak password contains 6-15 characters, while a strong password has 16-23 characters.

Here is a list of recommendations for using characters to create secure passwords:

1. Include Symbols (e.g. @#$%)
2. Numbers (e.g. 123456)
3. Exclude Similar Characters (e.g. i, l, 1, L, o, 0, O)

58

4. Exclude Ambiguous Characters (e.g. { } [ ] ( ) / \ ' " ` ~ , ; : . < >)
5. Include Lowercase Characters (e.g. abcdefg)

There are several other things to avoid:

1. Same password, security question and answer for multiple online accounts
2. Use a password that has at least 16 characters, use at least one number, one uppercase letter, one lowercase letter and one special symbol
3. Use of names of families, friends or even pets
4. Postcodes, social security numbers, date of birth, house numbers, phone numbers, ID card numbers, etc.
5. Dictionary words
6. Two or more similar passwords which most characters are same
7. Anything that can be cloned (but can't be changed), such as fingerprints
8. Logging in to important accounts on the computers of others, or when connected to a public Wi-Fi hotspot

Furthermore, you should not let your Web browsers store your passwords (especially on public computers), since all passwords saved in Web browsers can be revealed easily. So ignore the message that asks you to save your password! You should close your web browser when you are away from your computer, because the cookies can be intercepted with a USB device or other means. Consequently, it is possible to bypass verification and log into your account with those stolen cookies on other computers. I would also advise that if you are on vacation and you leave your room with a computer and/or mobile device still there, that you find ways to lock them.

Chapter 7
Social Media Settings

Section Topics

- ❖ Social Media Settings
- ❖ Business Risk
- ❖ Combating Cybersecurity Issues
- ❖ Facebook
- ❖ Twitter
- ❖ LinkedIn

Social Media Settings

Safe social media use is the No. 1 cybersecurity challenge for employees, according a Wombat Security Technologies report, pertaining to security awareness issues in enterprise organizations. Hundreds of security professionals were surveyed from variety of sectors, including finance, technology, healthcare and education. After social media, the least understood cybersecurity topics across all industries were data protection, identifying phishing threats, protection of confidential information, and work safety outside the office.

Social media is a place where people tend to let their guard down. On sites such as Facebook, Instagram, Twitter, and LinkedIn, where the atmosphere is casual, users can let certain information slip, which consequently, brings risk. The information that employees and average citizens post to social media can be used against them, and in various cases, has. Social media in an effective tool to socially engineer targets; what you publicly tweeted about can be used to craft a targeted phishing email containing a malicious link. A picture on the internet gets saved into multiple locations. Furthermore, there is even a website that essentially takes copies of other websites, called the Wayback Machine (https://archive.org/web/)

Source: archive.org/web/

The point of becoming aware is not to become fearful or paranoid, but to simply to become more aware. Businesses, schools, media, and society as a whole are becoming increasingly more digital and technologically advanced. Therefore, it is incumbent on us to be diligent in making cybersecurity a top priority, particularly as social media has become an essential tool of communication.

Business Risk

Various pitfalls associated with social media use are widely known, but there are many potential risks for businesses that are less understood. Employees can overshare documents, which provide unnecessary access to corporate accounts and security controls. Employees' email addresses are often scoured, thus, phishing emails or ransomware could be directed to any organization.

One of the first steps to solving the problem is coming to the realization that social media will always be susceptible to attackers. Ways to reducing the potential of attacks include educating employees on how much they should expose on social media, in addition to finding the best use of available privacy settings. Effective and robust social media policies will incorporate security concerns as well as password guidelines and determining who can access the accounts.

Combating Cybersecurity Issues

A social media policy and training are the best tools to combat cybersecurity issues as these platforms become increasingly prominent in businesses. A social media manager should be tasked with maintaining, monitoring and administrating various social media accounts. This is especially advisable for smaller organizations that may not have a dedicated social staff. However, there are still security risks with having one person oversee social media accounts and activities. The social media manager can mix personal with professional. If the sole administrator has their personal account attached to corporate accounts, when their personal account is hacked, the danger naturally extends to the boss and other employees. When one computer is attacked in a network, other connected computers become at risk of getting attacked as well. Security can be threatened, as well as the brand image. Inflammatory tweets coming from a corporate account could push clients away and lead to negative media attention.

One person should be designated as the "main administrator," but other employees (stakeholders, executives, human resources, marketing department, etc.) should have access to the social media information available. Passwords to all of the corporate accounts need to be in a shared password manager. Employees should be discouraged from attaching their personal accounts to professional accounts.

Facebook

Cyber criminals have developed a trick for Facebook users called account cloning. They are fooled into thinking that their account is hacked, but in reality, someone creates a copy of an account by using a name and photos copied from an account. They are able to block you so you can't see or report them. Then they send friend requests to users' Facebook friends. These criminals are scammers that con friends into accepting their requests, thinking it is someone they know. The scammer then tries to con them out of money stealing their identity to gain their trust. To clone accounts, scammers can add people as friends in order to see and copy personal details and private photos.

The first thing you can do is post on your Timeline, warning all your friends not to accept any friend requests that appear to be from you. They should report the friend requests as unwanted, which may get the scammer blocked from sending more requests.

You should also warn your friends not to believe any messages which appear to be from you, telling them they have won some lottery or other prize/grant. This is one of the scams these clones run, called the Advance Fee Fraud. You should be careful about who you accept as "friends"; settings should be set to ensure that only people you truly know can see your more private content. You should also make sure that when someone sends you a friend request, they can only send the request be confirming that they know you.

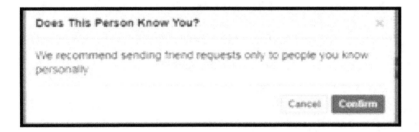

Users should go through their privacy settings and prevent their friends list from being public, because scammers will use it to target your friends. Wherever possible, profile pictures should be made private.

Twitter

If you are a Twitter user, you need to be mindful of how much information you share on Twitter or any other website. Information you consider to be private (i.e. credit card number or home address) should not be provided publicly. Similarly as anywhere else online, there should be avoidance of communication that asks for your private contact information, personal information, or passwords. The definition of what is considered private and what should be shared varies on Twitter, depending on the user. In the event that a friend or connection posts private information, you should contact them and ask them to take down the content.

Twitter provides login verification for users to enforce, which is an extra layer of security for accounts. Rather than only using a password, login verification introduces a second check to help make sure that you, only the user can access his or her Twitter account. Only people who have access to your password and mobile phone can log in to your account.

Here is a link for instructions on how to use login information on Twitter: https://support.twitter.com/articles/20170388

Phishing is a common tactic used by hackers and scammers on Twitter to obtain usernames, email addresses and phone numbers. Whenever you enter your Twitter password, you should make sure that the URL in the address bar says twitter.com. If you receive a Direct Message (DM) with a URL that looks odd, it is highly recommended not to open the link, even if the message is coming from a friend. Twitter domains always have https://twitter.com/ as the base domain.

Password strength is important on Twitter. Users should create a strong and unique password for their accounts, as well as the email address associated with those Twitter accounts. The password needs to be at least 10 characters long, with a mix of uppercase, lowercase, numbers, and symbols. A different password for each website you visit. You can consider using password management software to store your login information securely. As in general online, personal information in your password such as phone numbers and your birth date should completely be avoided, along with common dictionary words such as "password", "student", etc. Another general rule that applies on Twitter is not to reuse passwords across websites. The Twitter account password should be unique to Twitter.

LinkedIn

On LinkedIn, users typically get connection requests from people that they do not know personally. Some connections are important to have pertaining to business and employment opportunities, but there should be caution with whom you add on LinkedIn. There are requests that originate from obviously fake profiles. This is likely intended for phishing campaigns, which are among the most popular means to acquiring security credentials and personal data.

There are dozens of fake LinkedIn accounts created by posing as corporate headhunters, who hunt for working professionals in industries such as telecommunications and government agencies. Users are enticed into giving up information such as business emails, which are major targets by hackers. Once the phishing campaign is completed, the employees' sensitive data could be used for fellow phishing campaigns.

Many LinkedIn users seek better employment opportunities or, at the very least, to catch the eye of a recruiter. Therefore, cyber criminals insidiously pose as recruiters to gain the trust of LinkedIn users. Several of the fake accounts become successful in networking – one reportedly had up to 500 contacts. Some even managed to get endorsements from others." At one point, Dell's counter-threat unit had identified at least 25 fake profiles, which had links to over 200 legitimate LinkedIn profiles. The epidemic of fake profiles has become so significant that BBC published a story covering a report via security firm Symantec.

One of the ways to combat phishing campaigns and fake LinkedIn accounts is through employee awareness training. Another good practice is to seek out confirmation about the individual by contacting the person's employer directly, or by Googling the person's name.

By default, all LinkedIn members who have your phone number have the ability to discover and connect with you. Therefore, you should consider managing how people who have your phone number are able to connect with you. That option is available under Privacy Controls.

You can also manage how people who have your phone number connect with you, by changing the default setting, which is All LinkedIn Members. But the best thing to do is not to list your phone number at all on LinkedIn.

Basics

Email addresses

Add or remove email addresses on your account

Phone numbers

Add a phone number in case you have trouble signing in

You haven't added any phone numbers yet.

Your phone number helps us keep your account secure. It also helps people who already have your number discover and connect with you.

Add phone number

Change password

Regardless of whether a user has an account on LinkedIn or not, anyone with Internet access can see your public profile. By default, LinkedIn makes all aspects of your profile visible to the public. Therefore, you'll want to make some adjustments to protect your privacy.

Under your LinkedIn page:

Me -> Settings & Privacy -> Privacy -> Edit Your Public Profile

Account	Privacy	Communications

Basics		
Partners and Third parties	**Basics**	
Subscriptions	**Email addresses**	Change
Account	Add or remove email addresses on your account	1 email address
	Phone numbers	Change
	Add a phone number in case you have trouble signing in	0 phone numbers
	Change password	Change
	Choose a unique password to protect your account	Last changed: June 27, 2017
	Language	Change
	Select the language you use on LinkedIn	English
	Name, location, and industry	Change
	Choose how your name and other profile fields appear to other members	
	Where you're signed in	Change
	See your active sessions, and sign out if you'd like	3 active sessions
	...ed preferences	Change

https://www.linkedin.com/psettings/change-password

As in general on the Internet, you should sign out of your account after you use a publicly shared computer. You should put your email address, home address, or phone number in the Summary area. Ideally, you only should accept connections from people you know and trust, or those you have common career connections with.

One option that can be considered is turning two-step verification on for your account. This requires a person to use more than one form of verification to access an account, usually via passwords and mobile devices. By turning on two-step verification for an account, LinkedIn requires an account password and a numeric code sent to your phone whenever the device you're attempting to sign in from is not recognized. Two-step verification helps to significantly reduce identity theft and unauthorized access to sensitive information, because most accounts can be compromised from unknown computers and devices.

Chapter 8
Real Life Experiences with Cybersecurity Issues

Section Topics

❖ **Cerber Ransomware**

❖ **SmartService**

❖ **Restore Disks and New Operating System**

❖ **Identity Theft**

❖ **Chromium**

❖ **Palikan**

❖ **Windows 10 Under Attack**

Cerber Ransomware

Cerber is a ransomware-type malware that infiltrates systems and infects various file types, including .jpg, .doc, .raw, .avi, etc. Cerber adds a .cerber (and in some cases .cerber2 or .cerber3) extension to each encrypted file. There are also variants of this ransomware that add a .beef extension to encrypted files. Following successful infiltration, Cerber demands a ransom payment from unsuspecting users to decrypt these files. There are messages that state that the payment of the ransom must fall within the given time frame (seven days), or the fee will double. Cerber usually arrives via an email attachment, using sense-of-urgency tactics to trick users into opening a Word file that will download and install the deadly Cerber ransomware. It plays on everyone's fear of getting billed for items they haven't purchased or for payments that were missed.

Cerber creates three different files (**#DECRYPT MY FILES#.txt**, **#DECRYPT MY FILES#.html**, and **#DECRYPT MY FILES#.vbs**) containing payment instructions. Once the e-mail is opened, and the document is downloaded, virtually all of the remaining files on your computer contain a .cerber file extension. Here is an example of its attack on the Pictures folder.

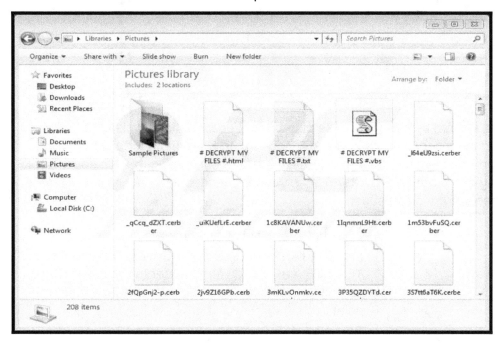

Source: pcrisk.com/images/stories/screenshots201602/cerber-ransomware-folder.jpg

I was fooled into thinking one day that an email was important. The email convincingly stated that I owed Yahoo a payment. I clicked on the email and saw a Word document attached. When I opened the document, the page contained a series of numbers, letters and symbols. Lo and behold, my computer was infected with cerber ransomware. All of my documents, music files, pictures and program files had the .cerber extension.

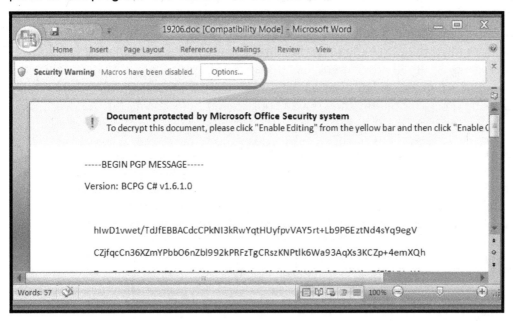

I did not want to do a system recovery because of important documents and files that were installed. Therefore, I did a search in various folders and in the Start menu for any file with Cerber extension and I deleted each of them. This is very time consuming, but it helps to avoid a complete scrubbing of the hard drive. However, it is recommended to do a system restore, if one is available, when .cerber files appear.

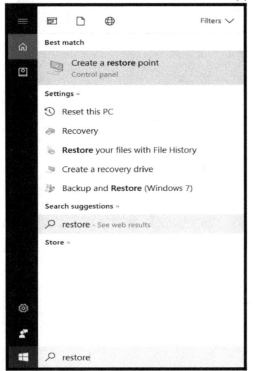

NOTE: Sometimes ransomware deletes restore points or blocks access to the System Restore function. This will be explained further later.In Windows 10, do a search for "restore", then click on "Create a restore point".

When the System Properties window opens, click System Restore

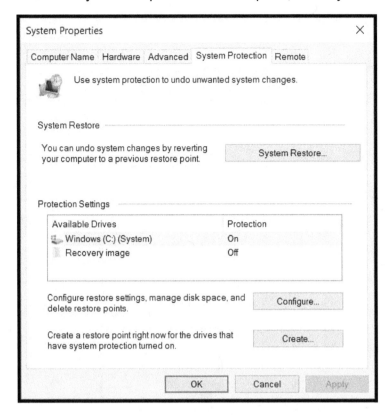

The System Restore window now opens. Click on Next.

If a recommended restore point appears, select it, and then click Next

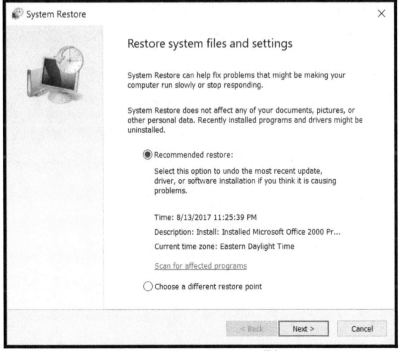

If the recommend restore point does not appear on the window, on the next page, you will find the available restore points.

Select the restore point that you want **(preferably most recent working restore point),** then click Next

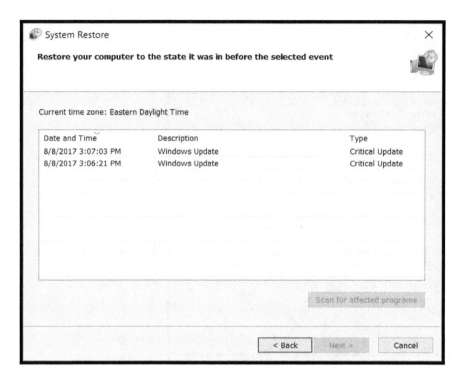

Click Scan for affected programs, and then wait

NOTE: Note that you can skip the scanning step and just click Next anyway, but it's always good to see what apps will be affected before you start the process.

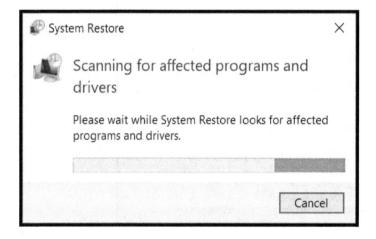

System Restore will then detect any programs that will be uninstalled during the process, and display two lists. The top list shows programs and drivers that will be deleted if you restore Windows to the selected restore point. The bottom list shows programs and drivers that might be restored by the process. It is important to note that even programs and drivers that get restored may not function properly until a full reinstall

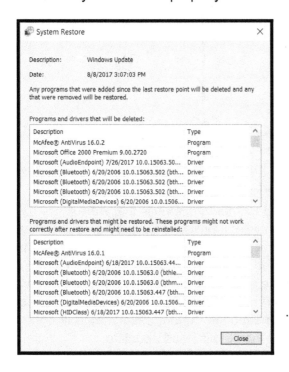

When you are ready to restore,

1. Click the restore point you want to use
2. Click Next
3. Click Yes
4. Click Finish

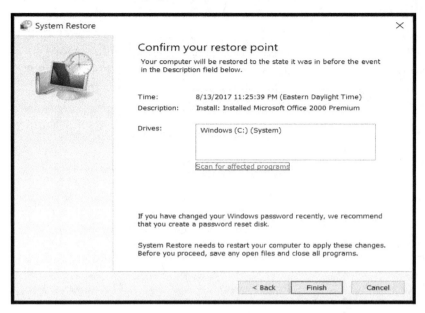

Users should always think twice before opening any attachments to emails that were unexpected, or look fishy (pun intended). Cyber criminals lurk online to sucker naïve users into accessing phishing sites, ransomware, and other viruses/malware via e-mails. You should make sure that the spam settings are optimal. Users also need to be wary of entering any information into a website accessed via an e-mail link; this could be a spoof website where your details are submitted directly to the fraudsters. For example, if there is an e-mail asking you to update your account details through a link, it is safer to access your account via your usual method (e.g. going on your own personal account) to verify whether the details need updating.

SmartService

My former Windows 7 PC started to experience significant issues. America Online and other program files would not open because of the following message:

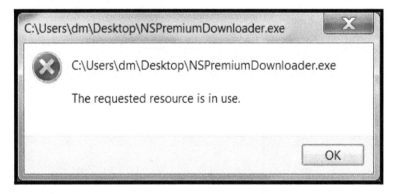

I then tried to open McAfee AntiVirus software installed on my system to no avail. After that, I attempted to do a system restore, only to find that the restore points were deleted. I cleared and backed up program files and documents in order to do a system recovery, but the system recover option was not available either. It was clear that my computer received a serious attack.

To make matters worse, the Cerber files also reappeared, even though I had removed them using the aforementioned deletion method. Therefore I had to find a way to remove this malware, and it was apparent that I had to find an alternate way of doing a full recovery. I did online research on the "The Requested Resource is in Use" error message, and found out that my PC was infected with a rootkit (collection of typically malicious computer software) known as SmartService. The message usually appears when trying to remove a particular application or perform a system scan with anti-malware or another security software. As I learned, it also blocks restore points and system recovery options.

Rootkits are far more severe computer infections than typical computer viruses; this particular rootkit can also be referred to as a SmartService Trojan. The malware roots deeply into the operating system, and modifies numerous settings. The stage is set to start performing malicious activities, including other virus infections and even identity theft. Rootkits are intended to operate silently, and to install malicious programs and files on the system, while being protected from being recognized and deleted. These Trojans infect the computer via unsafe links with suspicious online sources, as well as downloading/opening junk email attachments. SmartService also arrives through contaminated websites, such as free YouTube to mp3 download sites, where multiple pop-up ads appear.

Restore Disks and New Operating System

Since the system restore points were erased and the recovery options were blocked, I knew that I had to obtain boot disks specifically containing Windows 7. I came upon an inexpensive option on the Internet and obtained a package containing five system recovery DVDs, compatible with my computer.

My PC was working mostly fine for a couple weeks after I did the restore. However, one morning, when I turned it on, the hard drive was running, but the power light was still off, and there was no boot. Apparently the power supply or more ominously the motherboard was damaged by SmartService malware. My PC no longer worked. Therefore, I had to purchase a new PC; I decided on a refurbished one with the Windows 10 OS. This is proof that the ultimate damage from ransomware and other malware is destruction of computer hardware such as the motherboard and/or hard drive.

Identity Theft

In 2014, I discovered that my bank checking account was hacked. Two bogus checks for were written to a bogus name for over $1,000 each, which wiped out my account and put it in debt. One possibility that I have surmised is that I opened an account on a company web site to sell my e-learning products the very same week that my bank account was hacked. I Googled and did research about the company and I found out that other users have had bad experiences with this company as well. I was forced to open a new bank account, with a different routing number and account number, as well as a new debit card. I also made sure to be careful with the websites that I use my credit cards and bank account for.

If you are selling a product (books, t-shirts, clothes, food, etc.), it is advisable to do research on the company that you want to create an account for, even if it seems that you are getting a discount and/or more royalties. Additionally, here is a link to an article that provides advice for staying safe when selling online:

http://www.bankrate.com/personal-finance/smart-money/5-ways-to-stay-safe-when-selling-online/#slide=1

Furthermore, when speaking to employers, you should make sure never include your date of birth, social security number, driver's license number, bank account number, or credit card number. You should not include them on your resume, cover letter, or even in a phone conversation. This information should not be shared with any company until you have interviewed with the employer, AND been offered a position in writing.

Chromium

A fake Chromium browser has been unleashed to the public, getting installed unwittingly on many computers, with ulterior motives or purposes behind it. There is actually a real Chromium browser, but the program described here is an impostor designed to do something to harm your PC & privacy.

Chromium can be hard to stop from running on your PC, even when accessing the Task Manager or Change or Remove a Program option. I tried to remove Chromium using the latter, and the program was still embedded in the system. I would not advise installing one of the Chromium removers either, because those programs can sometimes cause additional software and/or hardware issues to your computer.

Chromium appeared unknowingly on my Windows 7 computer and then my refurbished Windows 10 computer. On the former OS, I thought it had appeared with a program that I installed, and I didn't consider that it could be a virus. In fact, I was actually using the program for an extended period of time. However, as mentioned previously, on one morning, I saw an outbreak of Cerber files on my system.

Chromium-based browsers are commonly distributed via a deceptive software marketing method called bundling, which secretly installs additional programs with regular software and apps. The fake browser often bundles with freeware or shareware from various download sites. For example, the fake Chromium browser can be downloaded with Flash Player Pro.

According to research, many users overlook potentially unwanted programs concealed within the "Custom" or "Advanced" settings. By rushing and skipping through the download and installation processes, rogue applications often are inadvertently installed. Therefore, it is imperative to pay close attention and analyze each step of the software download and installation processes. You should never accept any offers to install third party programs, or any extra program that you are unfamiliar with.

Palikan

Palikan is another browser hijacker that is bundled with other free software that you download off of the Internet. Free downloads do not always adequately disclose that other software will also be installed and you may find that you have installed adware without your knowledge. Once installed, it sets the homepage and search engine for any installed browsers to http://palikan.com without your permission.

This virus is very dangerous and can cause unnecessary damage to your PC. Palikan Search and Palikan.com covertly runs strange programs in the background to make the PC sluggish and at times frozen. Various system resources are consumed when it is running in the background. Palikan may also record browser history and cookies on the computer to help hackers steal money from victims. There is often a bombardment of pop-up advertisements, which can transfer users to illegitimate advertising sites or malicious sites. The Palikan virus serves as an effective way for remote hackers to take over control of your PC.

Besides the Chromium attack on my new PC, I also noticed the Palikan when installing the Internet Explorer 11. When I installed the program, there was an option to change the default search engine. My mother had recognized one of the two sites, which contained Palikan in the URL. Indeed, once malware infects the system, homepages and default search engines in Google Chrome, Mozilla Firefox and Internet Explorer are replaced by Palikan.com. There are actual legitimate programs that change these settings, therefore Palikan itself is not considered malicious. However, what is considered malicious is that http://palikan.com becomes attached to random Windows shortcuts on your desktop and Start Menu. It provides a faulty search engine with different ads and sponsored links that can redirect users to malicious websites. It is highly recommended to remove Palikan.com from your computer immediately.

It can be very difficult to remove Palikan Search and Palikan.com from the infected machine because related files constantly change their names to avoid being found. Removing the virus completely requires dealing with the registry editor, program files, .dll files, and various processes. It not only can deeply scan your entire system, but also can remove the infection automatically and safely with a few clicks.

If you have Google Chrome installed, one option is to remove Palikan.com by resetting the browser.

1. Start Google Chrome
2. Click the **Menu** button (three stripes) in the right top corner
3. Select **Settings** menu option
4. Find **Advanced** and click it
5. Scroll all the way down and click **Reset**

Make sure that you uninstalled the Palikan.com program, by checking **Search engines**, and clicking on **Manage search engines**.

After this, you should then remove the temporary internet files (Control Panel -> Network and Internet -> Delete browsing history and cookies).

It is also a good idea to invest in a anti-malware software to scan the computer for malicious and unwanted programs. There are also websites for Palikan removal that will provide information for fixing problems and protecting your computer against future malware infections.

Effects of the Palikan Attack

It was very evident that I was bombarded with attacks on my new refurbished PC, hours after it was delivered in the mail. As you can imagine, it was quite distressing to have lost one computer, and then have another computer encountering issues. However, I figured out that the issues were caused by what was a perfect storm of miscues:

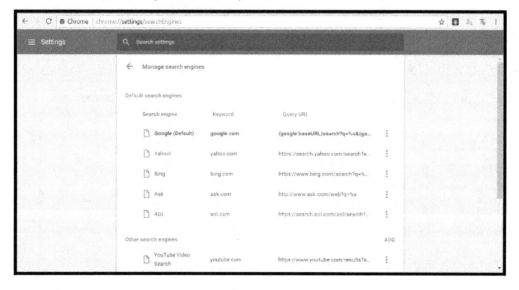

When I first activated the PC, I did not install an antivirus program initially. Instead I downloaded the following free software:

❖ I downloaded an mp3 file from a faulty site

❖ I attempted to install Flash Player Pro and IE11.

I subsequently determined that these websites were the source of the Palikan malware infection. In order to remove the malware, I chose the Reset the PC option. This option lets users return Windows 10 to its original state, without losing documents or personal files. This is the least invasive reset option, because users are able to retain accounts, personal files and personal settings.

To Reset the PC:

1. Click the Start Menu
2. Scroll down to Settings and click on it

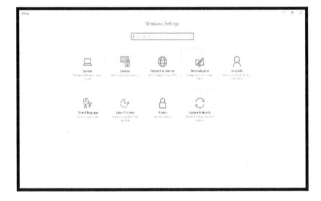

3. Click on Update & Security

4. Click on Recovery
5. Click Get Started, under Reset this PC,

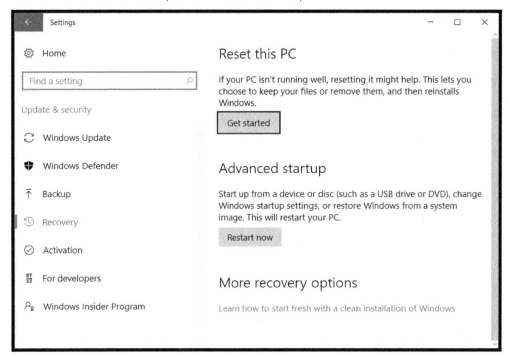

Precautions

I have learned valuable lessons with the cybersecurity issues that I have faced over the years. They have cost precious time and money, but something that I have gained that cannot be measured is knowledge and experience. I know now many of the pitfalls to avoid, and I want to inform all of the readers of this book who they can avoid them as well.

When speaking to business recruiters, I make sure not to give the last four digits of my social security number (SSN). I have stated that I will only reveal my SSN when I am assured of a job interview. As a matter of fact, a recruiter asking for any part of your SSN should immediately raise red flags about the validity of the recruitment, and what that person's real intentions are.

You should always make sure to pay attention when installing software because software installers often includes optional programs to install, such as the Palikan.com browser hijacker or Chromium. Users can opt for the custom installation and deselect anything that is unfamiliar (e.g. optional software never intended to be downloaded and installed in the first place).

One of the other ways of avoiding this attack is to make sure and install an antivirus program upon activation of your PC. Typically, a free trial of a program (such as Norton) is offered when the PC turns on; it would be wise to install the free trial, until you find an antivirus program that you are comfortable with. Installing the free trial also helps to ensure that you won't initially encounter an attack. Hackers and software pirates like to attack when a computer is activated to prevent product activation features from working, in addition to sabotaging the operating system.

Chapter 9
Network Security

Section Topics

❖ **What is Network Security?**

❖ **In Relation to Cybersecurity**

❖ **Home Networks**

❖ **Wi-Fi**

❖ **Network Protection**

❖ **E-Mails**

What is Network Security?

Network security is the protection of the file and directory access in a computer network against hacking, theft, and other unauthorized changes and attacks to the system. The access to data in a network is controlled by a network administrator. Users are assigned a unique ID and password in order to access information and programs and protect network resources. Network security covers a variety of computer networks, both public and private, for everyday jobs. Transactions and communications are conducted among businesses, government agencies and individuals. It is involved in organizations, enterprises, and various institutions. Not only are networks secured, operations being done are protected and monitored.

The network security team for a company, school, or university implements the proper hardware and software necessary to guard the security architecture. With the proper network security in place, any system can detect emerging threats before they infiltrate networks and compromise important data.

When network security is compromised, the first priority should be to remove attackers as quickly as possible. The longer they remain in a network, the more time they have to steal private data. According to Ponemon Institute's 2013 Cost of Data Breach study, the average cost of a data breach per compromised record in the U.S. is $188. Furthermore, the average total cost to an organization in the U.S. is over $5.4 million.

In Relation to Cybersecurity

Network security is a subset of cybersecurity that aims to protect any data sent through devices in your network. This is done to ensure that the information is not changed or intercepted. The role of network security is to protect the organization's IT infrastructure from cyber threats including viruses, worms, Trojan horses, Spyware, adware and other various attacks.

Difference between Network Security and Cybersecurity

To truly understand the field of internet security, it is important to note the distinction between network security and cybersecurity. Network security focuses on maintaining fortifications against outside threats, but its primary purpose is to guard against problems from within. Network security mostly protects a company's internal information by monitoring employee and network behavior in various ways. Essential tools for network security include IDs and passwords, firewalls, internet access, encryption, backups and scans.

Tools	Functions
IDs and passwords	Must be effective and updated frequently
Firewalls	Prevents outside threats
Internet access	Monitoring sites employees visit on company computers
Encryption	Ensuring that company information is not accessed outside the company

Backups	Saving company information in case of hardware malfunctions or successful outside attacks
Scans	Conduct regular virus and malware scans to detect outside infections

Cybersecurity focuses more with threats from outside. While network security is worried about what is going on within, cybersecurity watches to see who is trying to pass through the gate or security system. Though both areas have overlap, their areas of concern differ. Among other several important tools and functions, effective cybersecurity thrives with proper network protection, up-to-date information, intelligence, and applications.

Tools	Functions
Network protection	Detecting and preventing outside attempts to get into a network
Up-to-date information	Staying informed on efforts by attackers and hackers
Intelligence	Identifying sources of attacks and protecting against them
Applications	Monitoring of applications to avoid accidental breaches from within

Home Networks

A home network is a group of devices (i.e. computers, game systems, printers, mobile devices, etc.) that connect to the Internet and each other. The two most common home networks are:

❖ Wired network - connects devices like printers and scanners with cables

❖ Wireless network - connects computers, smartphones, tablets without cables

Home networking allows users to connect to the Internet from multiple computers, game systems, mobile devices, etc. They can also access files and folders on all devices connected to the network.

For example, here on Windows 10, you find out information about devices and connections in your home network by going to Settings. To access Settings:

Click Start Menu -> Settings

By clicking on Devices, you can see all of the devices connected to the PC, make adjustments to the settings for each device.

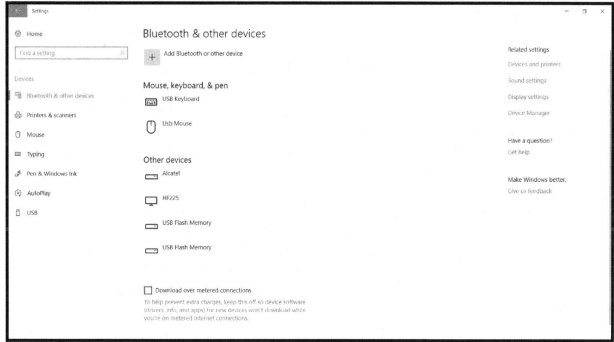

When you click on Network & Internet, you can see the network status (whether your PC is connected), along with other available networks and connections.

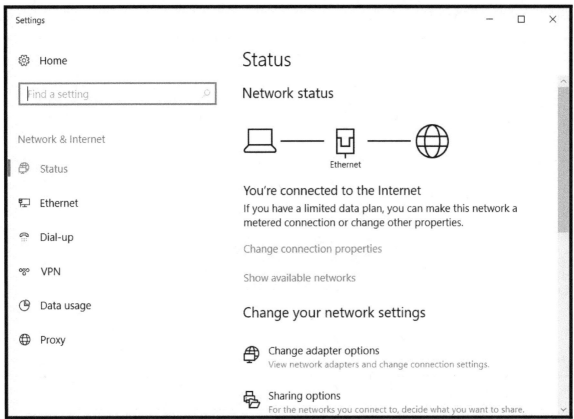

Home networks also allow users to print from multiple computers on a single printer, as well as manage security settings for each networked device.

Home Routers

Home routers facilitate this broadened connectivity on the Internet, including areas such as home-based businesses, telework, schoolwork, social networking, entertainment, and personal financial management. Most routers are preconfigured at the factory and are Internet-ready for immediate use upon installation. The Wireless Network Name (SSID) and password are required (usually found behind or on the side of the router) to activate the router. After installing routers, users often connect immediately to the Internet without additional configuration necessary.

Home routers are directly accessible and easily accessible from the Internet and are usually continuously powered-on, barring any kind of outage. However, routers are frequently vulnerable because of their default configuration, offering intruders an easy and ideal target to obtain personal or business data. Users are often reluctant to put configuration safeguards because of assumed difficulties or required time for advanced configuration settings. This, along with the wireless features provided in many of these devices could further add to the vulnerability.

Wi-Fi

Wireless home network security should be a top priority for anyone who has a wireless home network. Leaving your network unprotected could lead to consequences such as neighbors enjoying free Internet access at your expense or identity theft. Traditional wired networks are difficult for someone to steal bandwidth; however, the problem with wireless signals is that others can access the Internet using your broadband connection from a neighboring building or even sitting in a car nearby. This practice is known as piggybacking. It causes issues such as increasing your monthly Internet bill, decreasing the Internet access speed, and creating a security hazard by hacking and accessing personal files.

Protecting Wi-Fi

There are various effective ways protect to a wireless home network, many of which will be discussed later in this chapter:

❖ Protect your network from viruses and spyware

❖ Change your router password if the factory default setting hasn't been changed

❖ Use the strongest network security encryption compatible with each of your network devices

❖ Use firewall software

❖ Turn off your wireless network if gone for long periods (i.e. trip or vacation)

In the event that you forget your password to a wireless network, there is a way that you can connect without using a password. This is possible as long as the router supports Windows Connect Now (WCN) or Wi Fi Protected Setup (WPS). Here are the steps:

1. Click on Start Menu
2. Go to Settings -> Network & Internet

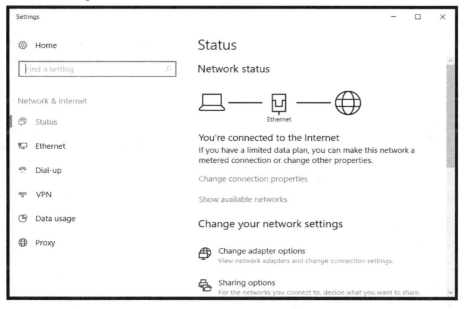

3. Click on Show available networks
4. Select the network you want to connect to and select Connect
5. Press the Wi-Fi Protected Setup (WPS) button on the router

The router will then be set up to connect to the network and apply the network's security settings. You will not be asked to provide a wireless network password.

Network Protection (CIA)

Strong enforcement provides the CIA with that ability to network traffic flows online. The process is started by classifying traffic flows by application, user and content. All of the applications must first be identified by the firewall. Proper application identification and policy management can be simplified by identifying and inspecting applications and their use to user identities.

(The concept of defense in depth emphasizes that the network should be secured in layers. These layers apply various security controls to sift out threats attempting to enter the network: access control, identification, authentication, malware detection, encryption, file type filtering, URL filtering, and content filtering.

Each of the layers are built through firewalls (the foundation of network security), intrusion prevention systems (IPS) and antivirus tools. These are effective tools for scanning content and preventing malware attacks.)

However, providing CIA of network traffic flows is difficult to accomplish with traditional firewall technology due to operations developed to bypass the controls. Traditional firewalls also assume that the IP address equates to user identity. Next-generation firewalls retain access control missions, but has enhanced the technology. Traffic across all ports are observed, and applications and their content are classified. Additionally, employees are identified as users, which enables access controls to enforce the IT security policy applicable to each employee of the organization, without a compromise in security.

E-Mails

Email security describes the various techniques used for keeping sensitive information in email communication, as well as securing accounts against unauthorized access, loss, or compromise. It also describes the process of using email encryption to send messages only to the intended recipient. Email security protects against ransomware, spoofing, and phishing.

Spam and Malware

Malware is frequently spread via e-mail on home networks and computers in general. They are often disguised to appear to come from someone you know and trust. E-mail also has threats from spam, spoofing, and phishing attacks.

Spam is a major e-mail security threat. Spammers obtain e-mail addresses from newsgroups, Web site operators, and malware that steals e-mail addresses from hacked e-mail accounts. Spammers even are able to successfully guess e-mail addresses.

As covered in this book, spam causes a number of issues for computers and users; it also causes headaches for e-mails as well. Staggeringly, spam can make up as much as 95 percent of all e-mails on the Internet! Spam can cause network congestion, as well as distraction and clutter. Spam can account for a large volume of e-mails, therefore, legitimate e-mails can get buried in the inbox and/or inadvertently deleted. A substantial amount of spam contains malware, or links to Web sites with malware.

The best protection against spam is to use a spam filter. For example, the Spam Settings page in the AOL Desktop Software allows adjustments of the level of spam filtering and the frequency of notifications of new messages in the Spam folder. Most browsers offer the ability to select an email, and then click the Report Spam or This is Spam button. The email will then be moved to the Spam folder.

Spoofing

E-mail spoofing occurs when an attacker sends users a fraudulent e-mail pretending to be a friend, relative, or someone they know. E-mail spoofing is actually easy to do, and is difficult to trace to the real sender. You should always be leery of any e-mail you receive asking for money or sensitive information, even if it appears to be from someone you know and trust.

Phishing

Phishing e-mails are a favorite weapon of identity thieves, as they are increasingly difficult to spot. They purport to be from a banking or other financial institution, as well as sites such as PayPal. Criminals also send an e-mail pretending to be from your bank. Phishing e-mails appear to be authentic, often including graphics and logos actually from your bank, and a link to the bank's actual Web site. But buried in that e-mail is a malicious link. Even without entering personal information, clicking the link can infect your computer with malware.

Identity Theft

There are various procedures to reduce your risk of becoming a victim of identity theft. You should never click on a hyperlink in a suspect e-mail, nor reply to a phishing e-mail with personal information (social security numbers, account numbers, passwords, date of birth, etc.).

You should look for grammatical errors in the e-mail, though identity thieves are getting more sophisticated. It is advisable to contact your bank via the number from your bank's Web site (NOT from the e-mail) if you suspect fraud. You also should check for any unusual or unfamiliar charges on your financial statements.

Chapter 10
Conclusion

Section Topics

❖ **Setbacks in Cybersecurity**

❖ **Progress**

❖ **Advice and Suggestions**

Setbacks in Cybersecurity

The fight for cybersecurity and against hacking will likely forge on for decades, as technology evolve and continues to become an essential part of society. The US government, tech companies, and other governments have collaborated and worked amongst themselves for comprehensive solutions to combat hacking and foreign interference. Furthermore, progress has been made over the last few years with the enforcement of various rules and involvement of the judicial system. However, as the Equifax scandal shows, cyber criminals will always find new and innovative ways to operate. In this concluding chapter, we will examine the setbacks and progress in cybersecurity, and detail advice and suggestions for businesses and users.

Equifax

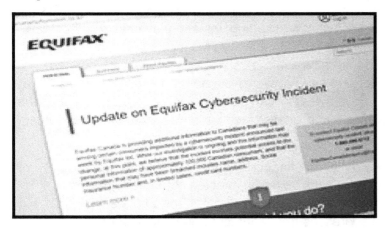

Equifax Inc. is a consumer credit reporting agency that collects and aggregates information on over 800 million individual consumers and over 88 million businesses worldwide. It is the oldest of the three largest American credit agencies (along with Experian and TransUnion, known as the "Big Three"), with over 118 years of service.

Equifax Inc. first learned about a major breach of its computer systems in March, which was nearly five months before the date it was publicly disclosed. The fact that this major agency suffered two major incidents in the span of a few months has added to a mounting crisis at the company, along with tremendous scrutiny and ridicule. Even when Equifax hired the security firm Mandiant with the belief of having the initial breach under control, investigators were forced back when suspicious activity was detected again near the end of July. The personal information of up to 143 million Americans has been breached.

Massachusetts Attorney General Maura Healey filed a lawsuit against Equifax over the company's failure to protect consumers' personal information. Additionally, more than 30 state attorneys generals, a U.S. Senate panel and federal authorities are investigating the company. The company has acknowledged that it had waited over a month to alert people to the breach; it potentially gave hackers the opportunity to access U.S. consumers' names, Social Security numbers, addresses, birthdates, credit card information, etc.

USA Today offered some necessary precautions to clients to safeguard their information. As mentioned before in this book, it is recommended to have strong and unique passwords, along with enabling two-factor authentication, effective antimalware, updating software, and backing up information. Another measure to consider is placing a credit freeze on your files, which makes it harder for someone to open a new account in your name.

Additional advice on what to do is on this link: https://www.consumer.ftc.gov/blog/2017/09/equifax-data-breach-what-do

Bots

Bots, or Internet robots, is an application that performs an automated task and gathers information. They are also known as spiders, crawlers, and web bots. Constructively, they are used to perform repetitive jobs, such as indexing a search engine, or completing orders. Bots are also used for automatic interaction with instant messaging, instant relay chat, or other web interfaces. However, they can also come in the form of malware. Malicious bots are self-propagating malware that infects its host and moves into a central server. Malware bots are used to gain total control over a computer and have a "worm-like ability" to self-propagate. One of the many unfortunate things about them is that they can easily go unnoticed. They hide in the shadows of a computer, creating file names and processes similar or identical to regular system files/processes.

Among other things, bots gather passwords, obtain financial information, launch Denial-of-Service (DoS) attacks, relay spam, and open back doors on infected computers. Bots are usually used to infect large numbers of computers, forming a "botnet," or a bot network. Spambots are also used to hijack email addresses from contact or guestbook pages. Bots can come in the form of downloader programs that suck bandwidth by downloading entire web sites, as well as website scrapers that grab the content of websites and re-use it without permission. Incredibly, bots are also used maliciously for buying up good seats for concerts, particularly by ticket brokers reselling the tickets. There are search engine spiders, which systematically crawl the Internet looking for new Web pages to add. They operate as chatbots, which hold conversations to accomplish a particular task. Crawlers usually consume resources on the systems they visit, as well as visit sites without approval. Schedule, load, and etiquette become significant issues when large collections of pages are accessed.

Increasingly over the years, bots have been used for spreading disinformation, political attacks, amplified perspectives, and sowing discord. For instance, Tay, was created as a teenage chatbot designed by Microsoft, billed as the "AI (artificial intelligence) with no chill". However, after a while, the bot wound up tweeting racist and offensive messages in response to other Twitter users. Microsoft stated that this occurred because of trolls that blatantly attacked the service. The negative presence and influence of bots came into prominence in the 2016 US election. The views propagated by these bots appear to be supported by a mass of real people. A recent study has warned that Facebook and Twitter bots are starting to influence our politics. In a testimony in front of the Senate Intelligence Committee, a former FBI agent described how Russians used Twitter bot armies to spread "fake news", using accounts purportedly from Midwestern swing-voter Republicans.

The report from Oxford University looked at the effect that social media bots posing as real users online had on the 2016 election. Researchers found that they affected the flow of information, with "the higher cores," which are the most influential networks of social media. The finding was that bots infiltrated these cores and significantly influenced on digital communication.

A patch is a piece of software designed to update computer programs and data, in order to fix or improve it. DeltaCharlie is a botnet malware used by Hidden Cobra (a North Korean hacking group) that targets computers missing certain patches. Thousands of computers worldwide by have been affected by DDoS attacks (Distributed denial of services attacks) on vulnerable computers. DeltaCharlie is capable of other attacks such as Domain Name System (DNS) attacks, Network Time Protocol (NTP) attacks, and Character Generation Protocol (CGP) attacks. Programs such as ManageEngine Desktop Central offer solutions where patches can be identified and patched automatically, and computers are protected from hazardous vulnerabilities.

Neighbor Spoofing

A rampant kind of robocalling has emerged called neighbor spoofing (or neighbor scam). These are automated calls from phone numbers that look strangely similar to numbers that are often called or received. From a personal standpoint, I really started to notice this tactic this year with my home phone and cell phone. Furthermore, my area code (Tampa, FL) ranks in the top 10 (at #10) for the top area codes affected by the neighbor scam. The number that appears on the ID has the same area code and prefix (first three digits) as your phone; commonly it is a telemarketer calling. This can happen multiple times per day, especially during the week. Callers are able to cleverly disguise their real phone numbers with a fake phone number with the same area code and prefix as a home or cell number; this is a way of tricking people into answering because they may think it is someone they know. Robocalls and telemarketers are the No. 1 complaint that the FCC has received from the public, and technology has made spoofing easier to enact and harder to detect. A hugely lucrative scheme for scam artists, people received approximately 2.5 billion robocalls per month in 2016.

Scammers use scare tactics such as making consumers believe that there is a warrant out for their arrest or that they owe the IRS money, in order for them to divulge personal or financial information. They often demand immediate payment, along with unusual forms of payment (wire transfers, debit cards, gift cards, etc). An app such as RoboKiller is useful app for blocking robocalls on your smartphone. The app uses a highly sophisticated and award-winning Audio Fingerprinting system that analyzes the audio of every spam call, even when numbers may be spoofed. The fingerprint analyzes the legitimacy and intent of the call, regardless of the phone number it appears to be coming from.

In my opinion, the best option to avoid falling victim to this scam is not to answer the phone if there is a number that you don't recognize on your caller ID. You should give them the opportunity to leave a voice mail message if it is important; this way you can verify the legitimacy of the call.

Petya

Petya is a family of encrypting ransomware, in which the malware targets Microsoft Windows-based systems. The master boot record is infected to encrypt a hard drive's file system table, preventing Windows from booting. There is a demand for the user make a payment in Bitcoin in order to regain access to the system.

Variants of Petya were first seen in March 2016, propagating via infected e-mail attachments. By June 2017, a new variant of Petya aided a global cyberattack (primarily targeting Ukraine, attacking over 80 companies), and propagates via the EternalBlue exploit, reportedly developed by the U.S. National Security Agency (NSA). It was used earlier in the year by the WannaCry ransomware. Kaspersky Lab also reported infections in France, Germany, Italy, Poland, the United Kingdom, and the United States.

Petya spreads via the Remote Desktop Protocol (RDP) and/or Server Message Block (SMB) protocols, which enable PCs and other devices to communicate with each other across a network. The ransomware usually displays the following message on an infected PC:

WARNING: DO NOT TURN OFF YOUR PC! IF YOU ABORT THIS PROCESS, YOU COULD DESTROY ALL OF YOUR DATA! PLEASE ENSURE THAT YOUR POWER CABLE IS PLUGGED IN!

CHKDSK is repairing sector xxxxx of xxxxxxxx (x%)

By installing a reputable anti-virus program, the Petya ransomware can be prevented and stopped in its tracks. It is recommended to obtain an anti-virus program that contains a Windows Security suite designed to 'auto update' and protect against the latest known variants of Petya and other global threats.

Wi-Fi Vulnerability (KRACK)

Researchers found a massive security flaw in Wi-Fi network protection, which could lead to theft of credit card details, private messages, photos, etc. The vulnerability affects ALL major devices and operating systems, including Android, Apple, Windows, Linux, and others. Researchers revealed details of an exploit (an attack on a specific system vulnerability) called KRACK (Key Reinstallation Attack), which takes advantage of Wi-Fi security vulnerabilities, allowing attackers to eavesdrop on traffic between computers and wireless access points. Up to 41 percent of all Android devices are vulnerable to a variant of the attack.

The United States Computer Emergency Readiness Team (US-CERT) has been alerted and issued a warning to the attack. It is recommended to install patches for all Wi-Fi clients and access points, when the fixes are available. For instance, Apple released macOS High Sierra 10.13.1, which is an update for the new macOS High Sierra operating system. The update includes a fix for the KRACK vulnerability in the Wi-Fi Protected Access II (WPA2) Wi-Fi standard, which protects many modern Wi-Fi networks. Other fixes will likely take time to roll out, and hardware vendors may encounter difficulty updating their products in a timely fashion.

National Security Agency (NSA)

The National Security Agency is the U.S.'s largest and most secretive intelligence agency. The NSA compiles massive troves of data on U.S. citizens and organizes cyber offensives against foreign enemies. However, according to a recent New York Times expose, it has been hacked, robbed, mocked, and deeply infiltrated by anonymous hackers. The breaching was performed by a group known as the Shadow Brokers, dating back to 2016. The brokers have posted cryptic, mocking messages towards the NSA. They have also sold cyber weapons to any willing buyer, including enemies such as North Korea and Russia. The Shadow Brokers had obtained many hacking tools utilized by the United States to spy on other countries. Critics and experts have questioned the NSA's ability to protect potent cyber weapons, along with the agency's protection of national security in general. There is indeed irony that an agency regarded as a leader in breaking into adversaries' computer networks glaringly failed to protect its own. Shadow Brokers have released the actual code and the weapons, the latter of which were created at huge expense to American taxpayers. The cyber weapons have been picked up by hackers from North Korea to Russia and used against America and other nations. Millions of people (including businesses) experienced their computers being shut down by ransomware, via payment demands digital currency for access to be restored. For instance, Mondelez International, the maker of Oreo cookies, had their data completely wiped off. FedEx reported that a European subsidiary attack delayed deliveries and cost $300 million. More egregiously, hospitals in Pennsylvania, Britain and Indonesia were forced to turn away patients.

Progress

In spite of the never-ending challenges and turmoil with cybersecurity, there have been many positive developments in this field. For instance, interest in cyber insurance and risk have spiked as a result of high-profile data breaches, as well as awareness of the exposure that businesses face. Ransomware countermeasures have developed, such as backups and recovery to secure electronic health records in the event that hospitals are hacked. Countermeasures also include a push-button solution enabling a securely hidden network to quickly communicate with a remote data center. Microsoft researchers have been working on various ways to augment the Windows Hello security access system via fingerprint readers or iris recognition devices. This increasing application of biometrics would effectively eliminate the need for passwords in the future. Cybersecurity experts are researching methods to apply real-time live security information and event management (SIEM) tactics through algorithms and active monitoring by humans. Digitally engineered personalities (DEPS) are futuristic constructs that are quickly becoming a reality. DEPs are equipped with a biometrics reader and VPNs that can connect an individual to an enterprise network (communications backbone that connects computers and related devices). This important for clinics and hospitals if the CEO is travelling and migration paths (high-level view of all the applications, technology and operations) need to be implemented for electric health records (EHRs). Instead of calling or texting, the CEO can simply activate the DEP to issue the needed approval. By 2020, the cybersecurity industry is expected to offer comprehensive solutions (such as the ones carried out by the National Security Agency (NSA) against mass surveillance and cyberwar. They will likely be in the same vein as the operation carried out by the NSA on a global scale.

The aftermath of the Edward Snowden crisis led to the investment by the NSA for millions of dollars in new technology and tougher rules to counter insider threats. The agency also has active investigations into at least three former NSA employees or contractors. The Shadow Brokers leaks have renewed a debate over whether the NSA should be permitted to use the vulnerabilities it discovers in commercial software for spying. The argument is that the NSA should immediately alert software makers so the holes can be plugged as soon as possible. The agency has maintained that it has shared with the industry over 90 percent of the flaws found, while reserving only the most valuable for its own hackers.

In May 2017, former FBI director Robert Mueller was appointed by the Justice Department as special counsel to oversee the investigation into possible Russian interference in the 2016 United States elections. Upon completing his FBI term, Mueller spent a year working as a consulting professor/lecturer at Stanford University, focusing on cybersecurity issues. Mueller's team and the Senate Intelligence Committee are seeking any evidence for financial dealings with Russia that aided Kremlin intelligence agencies to target email hacking and social media postings, which helped to undermine Democratic nominee Hillary Clinton.

In October 2017, executives from Facebook, Twitter and potentially Google testified in a House Intelligence Committee hearing on how Russians may have used social media to interfere in the 2016 presidential election. Facebook's General Counsel stated that an additional 16 million people had been exposed to Russian propaganda on Instagram since October 2016. This is in addition to the 126 million Americans who were potentially exposed on Facebook. In total, nearly 150 million individuals may have had exposure to the Russian effort.

The advances listed should represent the beginning of a larger strategy to keep individuals and corporations safe from cyber attacks, as well as prevent foreign entities from undermining the American electorate system. Lawmakers intend to use the hearings to give the public a clearer picture of how platforms were manipulated by foreign actors during the 2016 presidential campaign and beyond.

Microsoft says it has already fixed the problem for customers running supported versions of Windows. "We have released a security update to address this issue," says a Microsoft spokesperson in a statement to The Verge. "Customers who apply the update, or have automatic updates enabled, will be protected. We continue to encourage customers to turn on automatic updates to help ensure they are protected." Microsoft says the Windows updates released on October 10th protect customers, and the company "withheld disclosure until other vendors could develop and release updates."

Android and Linux devices have been significantly impacted by vulnerabilities, with attackers having the ability to manipulate websites. However, Google has promised a fix for affected devices towards the end of 2017 and beyond. Google's Pixel devices will be the first to receive security patch fixes.

Further Advice and Suggestions

Business and Users

Businesses should first think about what assets they're trying to protect from cyber threats before carelessly buying the latest security products. Such assets can include staff, intellectual property, customer database, and other important people and items. People should not be paranoid, but there should be a healthy awareness and understanding of the reality of cyberattacks. They often involve hackers trying to exploit gullible victims, such as employees responding to email phishing schemes; they are fooled into thinking the message is from a legitimate source. Users and businesses need to be skeptical not only of hackers, but from vendors that insufficiently secure their products. Technology also is never completely foolproof, including the software and internet services you use or buy. None are completely secure and hackers find ways to breach them. Even as advancements emerge in protecting data against hackers, they always will find ways to sneak through systems and attack. The only comprehensive way to protect systems is with cyber liability insurance that will help to stave off financial damage caused by such attacks.

Important and/or private data should not be provided on Facebook, Twitter, Instagram, or any public social media outlet. It can be stored in a cloud or media such as CDs and flash drives. Over the past half-decade, cloud computing has helped many enterprises transform their IT practices, with public, private and hybrid cloud services.

You should never leave your devices unattended, even at home. When your computer, phone, or tablet has to be left alone for any length of time, they should be put away in a private but reachable (to you) area. Passwords can also be installed for devices such as your PC, tablet, or smartphone. Any sensitive information on a flash drive or external hard drive should be put away in a specific area as well.

Users always need to be careful when clicking on attachments or links in e-mails. If they look unfamiliar, or are suspicious (such as demanding money unexpectedly for an account), under no circumstance should you click on it. Once I clicked on one of those types of e-mails and opened an attached document and learned the hard way. My computer got infected with ransomware and I lost a lot of data; fortunately I had a lot of important documents on flash drives and CDs. A way of checking for false websites is to look at the URL of the website for the link. Oftentimes criminals will make minor, but not particularly noticeable spelling mistakes.

Sensitive browsing (i.e. banking, shopping, logging into school or work accounts) should ideally be done on a device that belongs to you. In the event that you have to use a public computer (or computer in someone's home), and you are asked if you want the computer to remember your log-in information, always select "Never" or "No". And when you are finished, always make sure to log out of that account. You should particularly avoid entering your credit card number or social security number on a public network.

Security Programs

There are some effective Internet software programs (many with free trials) that can increase cybersecurity for Web sites and computers in general. Here is a list of some of the programs:

- ❖ AVG Secure Search
- ❖ AVG Internet Security
- ❖ Avast
- ❖ Spybot - Search & Destroy
- ❖ SpywareBlaster
- ❖ XP-AntiSpy
- ❖ X-Cleaner

Checking if Your System Is Malware Infected

These are alerts to let you know that your PC may be infected
1. SLOWDOWNS
2. POP-UPS
3. CRASHES
4. SUSPICIOUS HARD DRIVE ACTIVITY
5. RUNNING OUT OF HARD DRIVE SPACE
6. ABNORMAL HIGH NETWORK ACTIVITY
7. NEW BROWSER HOMEPAGE, NEW TOOLBARS, UNWANTED WEBSITES
8. UNUSUAL MESSAGES OR PROGRAMS THAT START AUTOMATICALLY
9. YOUR SECURITY SOLUTION SUDDENLY DISABLED
10. FRIENDS INFROM YOU OF STRANGE MESSAGES SUPPOSEDLY FROM YOU

To find out more about these steps, you can visit:

https://heimdalsecurity.com/blog/warning-signs-operating-system-infected-malware/

References

[NC4] (2016, Sept 13). NC4 Cyber Defense Solutions | What's it all about? Retrieved from
https://www.youtube.com/watch?v=BumV2LnlpYg

Agarwal, A. (2014). How to Secure Your Wireless (Wi-Fi) Home Network. Retrieved from
https://www.labnol.org/internet/secure-your-wireless-wifi-network/10549/

Alliance Insurance Group (2017). 5 New Advances in Enterprise Level Cybersecurity. Retrieved
from http://www.allinsgrp.com/blog/5-new-advances-in-enterprise-level-cybersecurity.aspx

Alliance of Automobile Manufacturers. Cybersecurity. Retrieved from
https://autoalliance.org/connected-cars/cybersecurity/

Andriotis, A. (2017). Massachusetts Attorney General Hits Equifax With Suit Over Hack.
Retrieved from https://www.wsj.com/articles/equifax-says-data-breach-possibly-affected-100-000-
canadian-consumers-1505834728

Australian Cyber Security Network. Retrieved from http://www.csns.co/

Bing, C. (2017). Researchers find link between cyber espionage group and Saudi hacking
campaign. Retrieved from https://www.cyberscoop.com/shamoon-greenbug-symantec-hacking-
campaign/

Bloomberg (2017). Company Overview of Cyber Security Network, LLC. Retrieved from
https://www.bloomberg.com/research/stocks/private/snapshot.asp?privcapId=384056131

Boulton, C (2017). 6 trends shaping IT cloud strategies today. Retrieved from
https://www.cio.com/article/3137946/cloud-computing/6-trends-that-will-shape-cloud-computing-in-
2017.html

Bowers, L. (2017). Neighbor Scam Surges 15x in 2017, Imitates First Six Digits of Phone
Numbers. Retrieved from https://hiya.com/blog/2017/07/10/neighbor-scam-surges/

Bradley, T. (2017). 4 Free Spyware and Adware Detection & Removal Software. Retrieved from
https://www.lifewire.com/free-spyware-and-adware-detection-removal-software-2487933

Breland, A. (2017). Facebook, Twitter, Google invited to testify on Russian election meddling.
Retrieved from http://thehill.com/policy/technology/354265-facebook-twitter-and-google-invited-to-
house-intelligence-hearing-on

Bronson, C. (2016). Proposed cybersecurity law for insurance firms has "fundamental
problems". Retrieved from http://www.insurancebusinessmag.com/us/news/cyber/proposed-
cybersecurity-law-for-insurance-firms-has-fundamental-problems-37787.aspx

Brsmst (2015). How to Wholly Remove Palikan Search and Palikan.com - Remove Redirect
Virus from Your PC? Retrieved from https://storify.com/mxzhd25wo/how-to-wholly-remove-
palikan-search-and-palikan-co

Brunk, M. (2017). Internet Security: Use Wisely. Retrieved from
https://www.nojitter.com/post/240172780/internet-security-use-wisely

Camp, C. (2012). Free YouTube .mp3 converters – with a free malware bonus. Retrieved from
https://www.welivesecurity.com/2012/07/24/free-youtube-mp3-converters-with-a-free-malware-bonus/

Cherrayil, N.K. (2016). Mobile devices to come under growing attack. Retrieved from
http://gulfnews.com/business/sectors/technology/mobile-devices-to-come-under-growing-attack-1.1825011

Cimpanu, C. (2016). Cerber Ransomware Spreads via Fake Credit Card Email Reports.
Retrieved from https://www.bleepingcomputer.com/news/security/cerber-ransomware-spreads-via-fake-credit-card-email-reports/

Cisco . Cisco Email Security. Retrieved from
https://www.cisco.com/c/en/us/products/security/email-security/index.html

Clover, J. (2017). Apple Releases macOS High Sierra 10.13.1 With New Emoji, WPA2 Security
Fix. Retrieved from https://www.macrumors.com/2017/10/31/apple-releases-macos-high-sierra-10-13-1/

CNBC (2017). Germany big target of cyber espionage and attacks: Government report.
Retrieved from https://www.cnbc.com/2017/07/04/germany-big-target-of-cyber-espionage-and-attacks-government-report.html

Collett, S. (2016). Can cybersecurity save the November elections? Retrieved from
http://www.csoonline.com/article/3116984/cyber-attacks-espionage/can-cybersecurity-save-the-november-elections.html

Computer Security Wiki. Grayware. Retrieved from
http://computersecurity.wikia.com/wiki/Grayware

Cyber Risk & Insurance Forum (2014). Cyber Security Risk in a Social Media World. Retrieved
from http://www.cyberriskinsuranceforum.com/content/cyber-security-risk-social-media-world

Cyber Security Network, LLC. Retrieved from https://cybersn.com/index.html

Cybersecurity Legislation 2016. Retrieved from http://www.ncsl.org/research/telecommunications-and-information-technology/cybersecurity-legislation-2016.aspx

Department of Homeland Security (2015). Security Tip (ST15-002) Securing Your Home
Network. Retrieved from https://www.us-cert.gov/ncas/tips/ST15-002

Doe, J. (2017). How to Fix "The Requested Resource is in Use" Error? Retrieved from
https://ugetfix.com/ask/how-to-fix-the-requested-resource-is-in-use-error/

Drapala, K. (2013). Top Ten: The Most Important Cyber Security Tips for Your Users. Retrieved
from https://umbrella.cisco.com/blog/2013/10/08/top-ten-important-cyber-security-tips-users/

Dwyer, C. (2017). Equifax Chief Steps Down After Massive Data Breach. Retrieved from http://www.npr.org/sections/thetwo-way/2017/09/26/553693826/equifax-chief-steps-down-after-massive-data-breach

ECPI University . ECPI Blog. Retrieved from https://www.ecpi.edu/blog/whats-difference-between-network-security-cyber-security

Entrust Datacard. Retrieved from https://www.entrust.com/3-ways-law-enforcement-can-strengthen-cybersecurity/

Farah, J. (2017). Moving Beyond Patch and Pray Cybersecurity. Retrieved from http://www.wnd.com/2017/04/moving-beyond-patch-and-pray-cybersecurity/

Federal Trade Commission (2017). Tech Support Scams. Retrieved from https://www.consumer.ftc.gov/articles/0346-tech-support-scams

Finn, P. and Horwitz, S. (2013). U.S. charges Snowden with espionage. Retrieved from https://www.washingtonpost.com/world/national-security/us-charges-snowden-with-espionage/2013/06/21/507497d8-dab1-11e2-a016-92547bf094cc_story.html?utm_term=.37c89eaea717

FireEye. Retrieved from https://www.fireeye.com/

FireEye. Why FireEye? Retrieved from https://www.fireeye.com/company/why-fireeye.html

Flamini, R. (2013). Is the United States safe from Internet criminals? Retrieved from http://library.cqpress.com/cqresearcher/document.php?id=cqresrre2013021506

Geller, E. (2016). Cybersecurity firm links state election hacks to Russian activity in Europe.

Georgetown Journal of International Affairs. Retrieved from http://journal.georgetown.edu/the-rise-of-hacktivism/

Glenn, W. (2016). How to Use System Restore in Windows 7, 8, and 10. Retrieved from https://www.howtogeek.com/howto/windows-vista/using-windows-vista-system-restore/

Goeij de, H. (2017). Czech Government Suspects Foreign Power in Hacking of Its Email. Retrieved from https://www.nytimes.com/2017/01/31/world/europe/czech-government-suspects-foreign-power-in-hacking-of-its-email.html

Gressin, S. (2017). The Equifax Data Breach: What to Do. Retrieved from https://www.consumer.ftc.gov/blog/2017/09/equifax-data-breach-what-do

Guest Writer (2017). The economics of cybersecurity for the undecided. Retrieved from https://www.welivesecurity.com/2017/03/22/economics-cybersecurity-undecided/

Guest_gacl_(2015). Is youtube-mp3.org safe? Retrieved from https://www.bleepingcomputer.com/forums/t/583993/is-youtube-mp3org-safe/

Hagen, L. (2016). Kerry: Russian interference had 'profound impact' on election. Retrieved from http://thehill.com/policy/cybersecurity/312010-kerry-russian-interference-had-profound-impact-on-election

Heddings, L. (2014). The "Tech Support" Scammers Called HTG (So We Had Fun with Them). Retrieved from https://www.howtogeek.com/180514/the-%E2%80%9Ctech-support%E2%80%9D-scammers-called-htg-so-we-had-fun-with-them/

Help Net Security (2017). The global impact of huge cyber security events. Retrieved from https://www.helpnetsecurity.com/2017/10/02/impact-huge-cyber-security-events/

Hoffman, C. (2014). What You Need to Know About Creating System Image Backups. Retrieved from https://www.howtogeek.com/192115/what-you-need-to-know-about-creating-system-image-backups/

Hosenball, M. (2017). FBI investigation into Donald Trump's ties to Russia takes on British spy's leaked dossier. Retrieved from http://www.independent.co.uk/news/world/americas/donald-trump-russian-election-hacking-fbi-special-counsel-robert-mueller-christopher-steele-spy-a7985876.html

Houser, S. (2017). Cyber security experts give tips on social media safety. Retrieved from http://fox59.com/2017/03/31/cyber-security-experts-give-tips-on-social-media-safety/

https://www.theguardian.com/commentisfree/2013/jun/22/snowden-espionage-charges

Instagram. I think my Instagram account has been hacked. Retrieved from https://help.instagram.com/149494825257596?helpref=related&ref=related

Instagram. What's two-factor authentication? How do I use it?. Retrieved from https://help.instagram.com/566810106808145?helpref=search&sr=1&query=security

JDP_1001 (2012). Event Viewer Scam (Phone Call). Retrieved from https://answers.microsoft.com/en-us/protect/forum/mse-protect_scanning/event-viewer-scam-phone-call/9c9c407c-592a-4e58-a2fb-32d3900154c3

Jenkins, A. (2017). What to Know About Former FBI Chief Robert Mueller. Retrieved from http://time.com/4783549/robert-mueller-fbi-special-counsel-donald-trump-russia/

Kan, M. (2017). Hackers Exploit Adobe Flash Flaw To Install Infamous Spyware. Retrieved from https://www.pcmag.com/news/356827/hackers-exploit-adobe-flash-flaw-to-install-infamous-spyware

Kan, M. (2017). Top Ten: The Most Important Cyber Security Tips for Your Users. Retrieved from https://www.pcworld.com/article/3171280/security/experts-at-rsa-give-their-best-cybersecurity-advice.html

Kiguolis, U. (2015). Cerber virus. How to remove? (Uninstall guide). Retrieved from http://www.2-spyware.com/remove-cerber-virus.html

KMVT (2017). . Gov. Otter issues executive order enacting Cybersecurity Task Force recommendations. Retrieved from http://www.kmvt.com/content/news/Gov-Otter-issues-executive-order-enacting--Cybersecurity-Task-Force-recommendations-410840145.html

Larson, S. (2017). Instagram alerts high-profile users their data may have been accessed. Retrieved from http://money.cnn.com/2017/08/30/technology/culture/instagram-hack-patch-bug-api/index.html

Law360 (2016). 3 Ways Cybersecurity Law In China Is About To Change. Retrieved from https://www.law360.com/articles/791505/3-ways-cybersecurity-law-in-china-is-about-to-change

Lima. A Short History of Cyber Security. Retrieved from http://www.lima.co.uk/blog/a-short-history-of-cyber-security/

Lockie, A. (2017). The US's most secretive intelligence agency was embarrassingly robbed and mocked by anonymous hackers. Retrieved from https://www.aol.com/article/news/2017/11/13/the-uss-most-secretive-intelligence-agency-was-embarrassingly-robbed-and-mocked-by-anonymous-hackers/23275398/

Loeb, L. (2017). Cerber Ransomware Owns the Market. Retrieved from https://securityintelligence.com/news/cerber-ransomware-owns-the-market/

Lord, N. (2017). What Email Security Data Protection 101. Retrieved from https://digitalguardian.com/blog/what-email-security-data-protection-101

Loriggio, P. (2017). Charges against Canadian arrested in Yahoo hack may be politically motivated: lawyer. Retrieved from http://www.nationalobserver.com/2017/03/16/news/charges-against-canadian-arrested-yahoo-hack-may-be-politically-motivated-lawyer

Malware-Detective.com (2014). How to Remove Palikan.com from Google Chrome? Retrieved from http://malware-detective.com/how-to-remove-palikan-com-from-google-chrome/

Mazzetti, M. and Lichtblau, E. (2016). C.I.A. Judgment on Russia Built on Swell of Evidence. Retrieved from http://www.nytimes.com/2016/12/11/us/politics/cia-judgment-intelligence-russia-hacking-evidence.html?_r=0

McAfee (2017). How to protect against Petya and other types of ransomware. Retrieved from https://service.mcafee.com/webcenter/portal/cp/home/articleview?_afrLoop=4454121799919743&_adf.ctrl-state=jpah5z3bq_4#!

Meskauskas, T. (2017). Cerber Ransomware [Updated]. Retrieved from https://www.pcrisk.com/removal-guides/9842-cerber-ransomware

Meskauskas, T. (2017). Palikan.com Redirect. Retrieved from https://www.pcrisk.com/removal-guides/8747-palikan-com-redirect

Meskauskas, T. (2017). Rogue Chromium Browsers. Retrieved from https://www.pcrisk.com/removal-guides/9570-rogue-chromium-browsers

Microsoft (2008). How to configure a computer to receive Remote Assistance offers in Windows Server 2003 and in Windows XP. Retrieved from https://support.microsoft.com/en-us/help/301527/how-to-configure-a-computer-to-receive-remote-assistance-offers-in-windows-server-2003-and-in-windows-xp

Microsoft (2016). Create a system repair disc. Retrieved from https://support.microsoft.com/en-us/help/17423/windows-7-create-system-repair-disc

Microsoft (2017). Add a device to a Windows 10 PC. Retrieved from https://support.microsoft.com/en-us/help/4028725/windows-add-a-device-to-a-windows-10-pc

Microsoft (2017). How to find your wireless network password. Retrieved from https://www.microsoft.com/surface/en-us/support/networking-and-connectivity/how-to-find-your-wireless-network-password?os=windows-10&=undefined

Microsoft. Five safety tips for using a public computer. Retrieved from https://www.microsoft.com/en-us/safety/online-privacy/public-pc.aspx

Miller, L.C. Types of Threats to E-mail Security on a Home Network. Retrieved from http://www.dummies.com/computers/computer-networking/network-security/types-of-threats-to-e-mail-security-on-a-home-network/

MIT Information Systems and Technology. Backing Up Your System. Retrieved from https://ist.mit.edu/security/backup

Mitroff, S. (2016). What is a bot? Here's everything you need to know. Retrieved from https://www.cnet.com/how-to/what-is-a-bot/

My Digital Shield (2015). A History of Cyber Security: How Cyber Security Has Changed in the Last 5 Years. Retrieved from http://www.mydigitalshield.com/history-cyber-security-cyber-security-changed-last-5-years/

Navarro, F. (2016). Don't have a Yahoo Mail account? Your data could still be leaked. Retrieved from http://www.komando.com/happening-now/374343/dont-have-a-yahoo-mail-account-your-data-could-still-be-leaked

NC4. 3 major areas of focus for modern cybersecurity intelligence. Retrieved from http://nc4.com/Pages/3-major-areas-of-focus-for-modern-cybersecurity-intelligence.aspx

NCSL Member Toolbox (2016).

NCTA. Cyber Security Network Meeting. Retrieved from http://www.nctechnology.org/events/overview/events/cyber-security-network-sep.aspx

Network Solutions. Online Security. Retrieved from http://www.networksolutions.com/education/email-security/

News (2017). What To Do if Your Social Media Accounts Get Hacked (and other Cyber Security tips). Retrieved from http://ovptl.uci.edu/2017/01/20/social-media-accounts-get-hacked-cyber-security-tips/

Norton . What are bots? Retrieved from https://us.norton.com/internetsecurity-malware-what-are-bots.html

Norton. About Norton. Retrieved from https://us.norton.com/about-norton

Norton_Team (2015). What is Spyware? Retrieved from https://uk.norton.com/norton-blog/2015/08/what_is_spyware_.html

NYU Center for Cybersecurity. Retrieved from http://cyber.nyu.edu/about/focus-areas/

O' Neill, E. (2017). Cyber Espionage and the Very Real Risk to Our Critical Infrastructure. Retrieved from https://www.carbonblack.com/2017/01/26/cyber-espionage-real-risk-critical-infrastructure/

O'Connor, G. (2017). How Russian Twitter Bots Pumped Out Fake News During The 2016 Election. Retrieved from http://www.npr.org/sections/alltechconsidered/2017/04/03/522503844/how-russian-twitter-bots-pumped-out-fake-news-during-the-2016-election

O'Neill, E. (2016). Hacking is the New Face of Espionage. Retrieved from https://www.carbonblack.com/2016/10/20/hacking-new-face-espionage/

Olang, K. . How to Use a PNY High-Speed USB Drive. Retrieved from http://smallbusiness.chron.com/use-pny-highspeed-usb-drive-52508.html

Pak, S. (2015). Apple Devices To Be Hacked More In 2016, Drastically Safer Than Android And Windows: Reports. Retrieved from http://en.yibada.com/articles/94717/20151214/apple-devices-hacked-more-2016-drastically-safer-android-windows-reports.htm

Palo Alto Networks . What is Network Security? Retrieved from https://www.paloaltonetworks.com/cyberpedia/what-is-network-security

PCMag. Antivirus. Retrieved from http://www.pcmag.com/business/directory/antivirus

Pegues, J. (2016). U.S. intelligence agencies release analysis of Russian cyber espionage. Retrieved from http://www.cbsnews.com/news/us-intelligence-agencies-release-analysis-of-russia-cyber-espionage-election-hack/

Pilici, S. (2017). How to easily remove Palikan.com Redirect (Virus Removal Guide). Retrieved from https://malwaretips.com/blogs/remove-palikan-search/

Policer Executive Research Forum (2014). The role of local law enforcement agencies in preventing and investigating cybercrime. Retrieved from http://www.policeforum.org/assets/docs/Critical_Issues_Series_2/the%20role%20of%20local%20law%20enforcement%20agencies%20in%20preventing%20and%20investigating%20cybercrime%202014.pdf

Press, G. (2015). This Week in Tech History: The Birth Of The Cybersecurity And Computer Industries. Retrieved from http://www.forbes.com/sites/gilpress/2015/11/01/this-week-in-tech-history-the-birth-of-the-cybersecurity-and-computer-industries/#75d741a76e4f

Price, R. (2017). There is a 'devastating' security flaw in Wi-Fi, and you're likely at risk. Retrieved from http://www.businessinsider.com/krack-attack-wi-fi-vulnerability-2017-10?r=UK&IR=T

Quora . Are there any safe YouTube to MP3 converters? Retrieved from https://www.quora.com/Are-there-any-safe-YouTube-to-MP3-converters

Restoredisks.com . Retrieved from https://www.restoredisks.com/

Retrieved from http://www.politico.com/story/2016/09/russia-hacking-europe-threatconnect-227685

Ricker, T. (2017). Wi-Fi security has been breached, say researchers. Retrieved from https://www.theverge.com/2017/10/16/16481136/wpa2-wi-fi-krack-vulnerability

Riley, M., Sharpe, A., Robertson, J. (2017). Equifax Suffered a Hack Almost Five Months Earlier Than the Date It Disclosed. Retrieved from https://www.bloomberg.com/news/articles/2017-09-18/equifax-is-said-to-suffer-a-hack-earlier-than-the-date-disclosed

RoboKiller (2017). Spammed by a Local Call? Here's How to Stop Neighbor Spoofing. Retrieved from https://www.robokiller.com/blog/local-call/

Rose, R. . How to Remove Chromium Browser from PCs. Retrieved from http://guides.uufix.com/how-to-remove-chromium-browser-from-pcs/

Rouse, M. (2005). computer exploit. Retrieved from http://searchsecurity.techtarget.com/definition/exploit

Saint, F. (2017). How to Delete Smart Service Trojan. Retrieved from https://www.malware-board.com/blog/how-to-delete-smart-service-trojan

Saltzman, M. (2017). Equifax data breach: Do a 15 minute cybersecurity makeover. Retrieved from https://www.usatoday.com/story/tech/columnist/saltzman/2017/09/17/equifax-data-breach-do-15-minute-cybersecurity-makeover/668684001/

Schneier, B. (2014). There's no Real Difference between Online Espionage and Online Attack. Retrieved from https://www.theatlantic.com/technology/archive/2014/03/theres-no-real-difference-between-online-espionage-and-online-attack/284233/

Scott, M (2017). Facebook Aims to Tackle Fake News Ahead of U.K. Election. Retrieved from https://www.nytimes.com/2017/05/08/technology/uk-election-facebook-fake-news.html?_r=0

Secureworks (2017). Cybersecurity vs. Network Security vs. Information Security. Retrieved from https://www.secureworks.com/blog/cybersecurity-vs-network-security-vs-information-security

SecurityScorecard R&D Department (2016). 2016 Financial Industry Cybersecurity Report. Retrieved from https://cdn2.hubspot.net/hubfs/533449/SecurityScorecard_2016_Financial_Report.pdf

Segarra, L.M. (2017). Facebook and Twitter Bots Are Starting to Influence Our Politics, a New Study Warns. Retrieved from http://fortune.com/2017/06/20/twitter-facebook-bots-politics/

SentinelOne (2017). The History of Cyber Security — Everything You Ever Wanted to Know. Retrieved from https://www.sentinelone.com/blog/history-of-cyber-security/

Shane, S., Perlroth, N., and Sanger, D.E. (2017). Security Breach and Spilled Secrets Have Shaken the N.S.A. to Its Core. Retrieved from https://www.nytimes.com/2017/11/12/us/nsa-shadow-brokers.html?utm_source=newsletter&utm_medium=email&utm_campaign=newsletter_axiosam&stream=top-stories&_r=0&mtrref=undefined

Shareef, T. . Fix Can't connect to the Proxy Server Error in Edge and Chrome. Retrieved from http://www.technicalnotes.org/fix-cant-connect-to-the-proxy-server-error-in-edge-and-chrome/

Shinder, D. (2011). What makes cybercrime laws so difficult to enforce. Retrieved from http://www.techrepublic.com/blog/it-security/what-makes-cybercrime-laws-so-difficult-to-enforce/

Shumsky, T. (2016). Business and Government Need United Cybersecurity Effort, Says Treasury's Raskin. Retrieved from http://blogs.wsj.com/cfo/2016/10/18/business-and-government-need-united-cybersecurity-effort-says-treasurys-raskin/

Starr, B. (2017). Federal criminal probe being opened into WikiLeaks' publication of CIA documents. Retrieved from http://www.cnn.com/2017/03/08/politics/wikileaks-cia-investigation/

Techopedia. Enterprise Network. Retrieved from https://www.techopedia.com/definition/7044/enterprise-network

The Backup Nut's Online Pulpit. USB Flash Drives as a PC Backup Solution. Retrieved from http://www.backupnut.com/flash.html

The Department of Homeland Security (2017). Combating Cyber Crime. Retrieved from https://www.dhs.gov/topic/combating-cyber-crime

The Federalist Staff (2016). What You Need To Know About Cybersecurity, WikiLeaks, And Bitcoin. Retrieved from https://thefederalist.com/2016/10/12/need-know-cybersecurity-wikileaks-bitcoin/

Thomas, D. (2014). EHR Migration Path. Retrieved from https://www.linkedin.com/pulse/20140904115346-34529931-ehr-migration-path

TSC Newsroom (2016). Two Ways to Improve Healthcare Cybersecurity Today. Retrieved from https://tscadvantage.com/two-ways-to-improve-healthcare-cybersecurity-today/

Uhrich, K. (2016). You've been hacked! 10 worst data breaches from Yahoo, and beyond. Retrieved from http://www.komando.com/happening-now/383579/top-story-youve-been-hacked-10-worst-data-breaches-from-yahoo-and-beyond

Ullman, G. (2015). Survey: CISOs see cybersecurity progress. Retrieved from https://www.fedscoop.com/the-cybersecurity-revolution-survey/

University of Miami Law School. Saving files to a USB drive. Retrieved from http://media.law.miami.edu/it/pdf/faq/back-up-instructions.pdf

US Department of Homeland Security (2016). Cybersecurity. Retrieved from https://www.dhs.gov/topic/cybersecurity

US Department of Homeland Security. Tips. Retrieved from https://www.us-cert.gov/ncas/tips

US-CERT (2011). Security Tip (ST08-001): Using Caution with USB Drives. Updated October 1, 2016. Retrieved from https://www.us-cert.gov/ncas/tips/ST08-001

Verizon. Wireless home network security. Retrieved from https://www.verizon.com/support/residential/internet/fiosinternet/networking/setup/security/124980.htm

Vinning, B. (2015). What is the security risk using Windows Remote Assistance? Retrieved from https://community.norton.com/en/forums/what-   security-risk-using-windows-remote-assistance

Wang, W. Steal this Computer Book 4.0: What They Won't Tell You about the Internet. Retrieved from https://books.google.com/books?id=nMwy2y_4VFcC&pg=PT96&lpg=PT96&dq=hackers+computer+activation&source=bl&ots=bgh8DtSDBP&sig=ipxpHC_x-LkclxV7g1-xLDH48sU&hl=en&sa=X&ved=0ahUKEwjJqaW05d7VAhWESyYKHeDVDgwQ6AEISzAH#v=onepage&q=hackers%20computer%20activation&f=false

Warren, T. (2017). Microsoft has already fixed the Wi-Fi attack vulnerability. Retrieved from https://www.theverge.com/2017/10/16/16481818/wi-fi-attack-response-security-patches

Wikipedia (2017). Biometrics. Retrieved from https://en.wikipedia.org/wiki/Biometrics

Wikipedia (2017). Computer security software. Retrieved from https://en.wikipedia.org/wiki/Computer_security_software

Wikipedia (2017). Cozy Bear. Retrieved from https://en.wikipedia.org/wiki/Cozy_Bear

Wikipedia (2017). Cyberwarfare by Russia. Retrieved from https://en.wikipedia.org/wiki/Cyberwarfare_by_Russia

Wikipedia (2017). Internet bot. Retrieved from https://en.wikipedia.org/wiki/Internet_bot

Wikipedia (2017). Internet security. Retrieved from https://en.wikipedia.org/wiki/Internet_security#Network_layer_security

Wikipedia (2017). Network security. Retrieved from https://en.wikipedia.org/wiki/Network_security

Wikipedia (2017). Patch (computing). Retrieved from https://en.wikipedia.org/wiki/Patch_(computing)

Wikipedia (2017). Petya (malware). Retrieved from https://en.wikipedia.org/wiki/Petya_(malware)

Wikipedia (2017). Robert Mueller. Retrieved from https://en.wikipedia.org/wiki/Robert_Mueller

Wikipedia (2017). Rootkit. Retrieved from https://en.wikipedia.org/wiki/Rootkit

Wikipedia (2017). Server Message Block. Retrieved from https://en.wikipedia.org/wiki/Server_Message_Block

Wikipedia (2017). System image. Retrieved from https://en.wikipedia.org/wiki/System_image

Wikipedia (2017). Tay (bot). Retrieved from https://en.wikipedia.org/wiki/Tay_(bot)

Wikipedia (2017). USB Flash Drive Security. Retrieved from https://en.wikipedia.org/wiki/USB_flash_drive_security

Wikipedia (2017). Vulnerability (computing). Retrieved from https://en.wikipedia.org/wiki/Vulnerability_(computing)

Wikipedia (2017). WannaCry ransomware attack. Retrieved from https://en.wikipedia.org/wiki/WannaCry_ransomware_attack

Wikipedia (2017). Web crawler. Retrieved from https://en.wikipedia.org/wiki/Web_crawler

Worthington, E. (2017). Is your phone spying on you? Creepy apps that can track your every move. Retrieved from http://www.abc.net.au/news/2017-10-24/spyware-apps-that-can-track-your-every-move/9042680

XFINITY . What is Home Networking? Retrieved from https://www.xfinity.com/support/internet/what-is-home-networking/

YourDictionary (2017). Network Security. Retrieved from http://www.yourdictionary.com/network-security